THE ROAD TO RENOVATIO

A GUIDE TO EMPOWERING THE MEANING-BASED WARRIOR FOR
INCREASED WORK/LIFE OPTIMAL PERFORMANCE

DR. MICHAEL D. AMOS

Published by Renovatio Group 2018

Book cover design and formatting services by Victor Marcos

www.renovat-io.com

ISBN
978-069207744-3 (pbk)

CONTENTS

RENOVATIO MEANING BASED WARRIORS ARE OPTIMAL LIFE ATHELETES

WARRIORS ARE:

A warrior is a person that leads a disciplined life that requires self-mastery and a way of being in the world that is beyond what ordinary people can manage. They focus on optimizing their lives through continual focus on discipline, preparation, self-mastery and skill mastery to perform life at an elite level.

THE RENOVATIO MEANING BASED WARRIOR

The renovatio meaning based warrior is a optimal life athlete.

LIFE

Committed to a meaningful existence focused on intentional living and the expectation of continuous internal growth regardless of the obstacles in their lives.

OPTIMAL

Focused on "Arête" or personal excellence. The meaning based warrior is a optimal life athlete.

RENOVATIO

ATHLETE

A disciplined person that utilizes ascetic practices to develop mental toughness in order to overcome their greatest obstacle which is the mind.

PREFACE

WHAT TO EXPECT FROM THIS BOOK

I wrote this book because I made a promise to my father that I would become a beautiful man, and I have found through all of life's struggles and setbacks that the beauty I sought was within me all the time. I just had to find the warrior within me. Now you may be wondering who this book is for. Well, it is for anyone curious about how to achieve personal greatness. Specifically, it is for the entrepreneur seeking to stay focused on his or her unique path; it is for the leaders that need to lead themselves before they can learn to lead someone else; and it is for the meaning-seeker who strives to be more than average. It is for the person who was like I was, needing to go searching for themselves. I tried to find myself by experiencing all my senses, but I remained incomplete. As you read this book, it is my hope that you get your mind ready for the hero's journey ahead. The journey is your personal path to greatness because the purpose of life is to leave behind some kind of legacy. It is your road to Renovatio, or the path of warriorship, which is a path to personal self-renewal and the reclaiming of personal power that is attained through self-mastery and skill-mastery.

More importantly, if you choose to take this path, you must recognize that you are your only roadblock; your life is a task, and you get out of it what you put into it.

In this book you will read about historical warriors who attained mastery in their work and their lives like Miyamoto Musashi. He was a Japanese samurai from the 1500s, his views are timeless and his *Book of 5 Rings* encapsulates mastery. You will also see the work of Viktor Frankl, who has influenced my scholarly work on coaching and work/life development, and of course you will see connections from Biblical warriors and the spiritual teachings of Jesus. As you are reading this book on warriorship, the concepts and the philosophies of the warrior come from various cultural views of the warrior archetype. All have been placed in the book for good reason. It is not meant to promote one spiritual view over another. While you will find references to a Judeo-Christian worldview, you will notice that concepts are derived from diverse schools of thought and that they are necessary in the process of communicating the essence of the material, specifically for understanding what it means to optimize performance, mental mastery, spiritual development, and the development of skill mastery.

However, the message in the book is very clear and much of the dialogue comes from my personal life experiences, performance psychology, athletic experiences, theories of psychology, and research taken from the fields of psychology, running, religion, industrial organizational psychology, and martial arts. The book is divided into four parts. The Book of Purpose focuses on assisting you in finding purpose and understanding human performance for human potential optimization. The Book of Self-Understanding details what is required to develop an understanding of who you are and challenges you to overcome yourself. The Book of Self-Mastery helps you to exercise personal power and build your will for increased performance. And the final book, The Book of Harmony, provides you with the way to work and live from a state of balance in order to attain the ultimate mastery by abiding in a place of love; because as you will find, the ultimate aim is to live life heroically.

It is my belief that one cannot explore any form of human or organizational performance if it is not done holistically because the common denominator of being human is being and becoming the better version of ourselves, which is the purest form of beauty. When faced with trials, do you view them as a curse or flip it and recognize they are meant to refine you and rebuild you stronger than before? The aforementioned questions are meant to get your mind reflecting on yourself from a place of truth and transparency. These questions will be covered inadvertently through the dialogue that naturally occurs between yourself and the reading. It is my hope that you will be blessed by the words of this book and begin setting new goals for your future. You are powerful. You are unique. Everything you will ever need is inside of you. Just to forewarn you, this book is about making a choice of taking the road to Renovatio, a process of personal renewal, the path of the renovatio meaning-based warrior.

Are you planning on staying where you are, doing the same thing you have always done, getting the same results as always before? Because we know what that is defined as... INSANITY! Are you ready to take this hero's journey, a journey through life that will make you a warrior? As I tell all my clients: Let's go get it! Let's go take your dream, and make it a vision, so you can live its reality! Let's go get it!

Sincerely,

INTRODUCTION

MY ROAD TO RENOVATIO

"Each night, when I go to sleep, I die. And the next morning, when I wake up, I am reborn."
—MAHATMA GANDHI

It was a little over eleven years ago that I realized I needed a reboot, a rebirth, or a renewal. I had lost my personal power and I had lost my path. In fact, my very first journal entry was titled *The Rebirth* and it was that first journal entry that began my new life and inner transformation. So, you are probably wondering where the term Renovatio came from? The name Renovatio is based on that very entry. I keep all my journals, so I can tell you the exact day I wrote that first entry: April 4th, 2005. Here is what the entry said:

> *"I begin writing this journal as a developmental book.*
> *In retrospect, I am ready to face my fears and flaws and*
> *conquer them. I just moved to Iowa after the collapse of*
> *my past life. In a sense, I died. I must say I felt like I failed*
> *when I left my old life, and I have promised myself that*
> *never again will I allow myself to accept mediocrity."*
>
> **— MICHAEL D. AMOS**

In order for me to create a path to excellence, I had to die.

That was the first entry and by far the most significant and courageous step I had ever taken in my life, because it began the process of writing my own magnum opus. It was on that day I began the journey to find the meaning-based warrior within me, who would begin the road to renovatio. That day I began viewing my life as a laboratory and I began to embrace the reality that life was uncertain, but even though it represented uncertainty, it was a journey.

The only problem was... I wasn't on the road to renovatio. I was like you maybe are right now. I was stuck. I had dreams, but I did not have a clear-cut vision of how to get there and at the time I sure didn't have the conscious mind required to get there. I walked in a dream state. That meant I was sleeping, even though I was awake. I was a zombie to my true potential. But life woke me up, and in order for me to become the better version of myself, I had to lay to rest my old life and get on with the journey ahead of me. See, before you can take a step forward, there are things you need to leave behind. The past must die in order for new life to begin.

Recently, over the course of his meaning-based warrior training, one of my coachees told me that he likened himself to a snake shedding old skin. The reason that transformative change does not occur for the most part is we are too afraid of the future and the desire to change is not compelling enough for us to move forward. It is not until a crisis occurs or we find ourselves at a point of no return that we realize our mindset needs to change. Trust me, I was sleep walking for a long time, but something woke me up. Life woke me up. Viktor Frankl woke me up. I remember the power of reading this quote by Viktor;

> *"Ultimately, man should not ask what the meaning of his life is, but rather must recognize that it is he who is asked. In a word, each man is questioned by life; and he can only answer to life by answering for his own life; to life he can only respond by being responsible."*
>
> **—VIKTOR E. FRANKL, MAN'S SEARCH FOR MEANING**

THE JOURNEY TO WAKEFULNESS

My wake-up call was the realization that I had not lived up to my responsibility to myself. Like so many people, I was fearful of change, yet I recognized that I was bored with my life. Have you ever noticed that when you are on a journey, you begin to see things differently? Your perspective on your life changes; and when you walk, you walk forward with excitement, although a bit fearful of the unknown. What you are truly fearful of is change.

Now let me explain how change works really quick. Change is the most frightening experience for a human being. Whenever I speak with a coachee, s/he always identifies change or the fear of change as a major issue. S/he recognizes that change is essential but finds it difficult. Most of us don't really know why change is so hard. Well, the truth is change requires something old to die so something new can take its place. In fact, change is a process, and interestingly enough the foundational research on the topic of change was founded by the work of Dr. Elisabeth Kübler-Ross, a Swiss-American psychiatrist and a pioneer in near-death studies. She was the author of the groundbreaking book *On Death and Dying*, a study in the field of grief and dying and identified stages that a person goes through when facing the prospect of death. She suggested that an individual experiences denial, anger, bargaining, depression, and acceptance, and her model of change has been adapted and used in change management and areas where individuals are going through life transitions. The point I am making is that change is a form of death required for new growth, and you should expect that you will go through these stages when you are seeking to transition or change directions in your life.

WHEN DID CHANGE OCCUR FOR ME?

I remember sitting in an apartment with no furniture, on a mattress, feeling very uncomfortable. I was journaling about the things I had lost, the direction I was headed, but I had no real idea of how I would get there. All I knew was that life had been calling me, and though I did not know how I would answer its call or whether I would arrive at my destination, I determined in my mind that I would move forward with courageous fear and I would work every day to become something more. My goal was just to be better than I was the day before, the week before, and the life before. I wanted to do more, be more, and achieve something more. Even though

I had no clue what that really meant, I just knew I had potential and it was going to take everything I had to bring it out of me. You are likely in a place of uncomfortableness. I was. But it is in that place of uncomfortableness, that place of obscurity that you must accept the death of your old way of thinking. What that means is you lack the self-awareness required to really know yourself, and this makes it difficult to self-direct your life.

But it is in this stage of obscurity that you will begin to learn what you are made of and embark upon the awakening process. It can be a very painful time, but once you begin to embrace it, you will discover your authentic person. The goal is to recreate yourself and find a direction that will lead you to your own personal renaissance. So start by asking yourself what life really means to you. What does it represent for you? Who do you really want to be? If you don't like things about yourself, you can change them. It is a matter of choice. After all, it is your life.

WHAT DOES LIFE MEAN TO YOU?

What life means for you, I cannot tell you. That is for you to figure out. But as I have said before, the definition of life is vitality. Vitality represents growth, and growth is a constant movement toward wholeness or well-being. It means to move, to act, to be, to become, to flow. It does not refer to being stuck, fixed, or lost in the past. Similarly, the process of life is a cycle. It represents life and death, and it is a balance.

Now, at the time, I did not understand the balance of my life. I don't even think I thought to look up the definition of the word "life." I only understood that my life was not what I wanted it to be, and I wanted so badly to be reborn. What I needed was to awaken spiritually to purpose. Because I had spent much of my life holding on to a past I could not change, chasing other peoples' dreams because I was too afraid to experience my own. I spent much of my life trying to acquire things I did not need and failed to accept and be mindful of the God-given talents I possessed.

Why do we devalue ourselves? I will tell you why. Because we spend much of our lives adopting the beliefs and views of others as our own. We may even tell ourselves that who others say we are is who we are, but the reality is you have to come to know your own person. You cannot rely on anyone else to define you. When you fail to realize who you are, you can never realize the potentials within you.

This is a typical problem I encounter when coaching clients. The problem I see with most individuals is that they acknowledge that life and moving forward are essential to growth, but they fear letting go of the past; they are afraid of relinquishing old beliefs and misaligned values because they have conditioned themselves to operate in that manner. Now they may say they want to change; but under the surface, they are comfortable with being complacent and frightened by the uncertainty of change.

Biologically, your body and mind adapt to a particular situation when you are continually exposed to a particular environment over and over and over. The body and mind just get used to certain circumstances. Let me give you an example: before my father died, he spent many years using an oxygen machine in order to breathe. The machine was so loud, and initially it kept us awake at night; but over the course of a few years, I remember we would have to turn the oxygen machine on just so we could sleep. See, our bodies became conditioned to think, feel, and adapt to our new and stressful environment. But it was difficult to unlearn.

If you want to take your business to the next level, if you want to take your career to the next level or transition to new heights of consciousness, something has to die so that something new can be born. The real problem is that most of us aren't willing to let go of the past and learn new patterns and set new expectations for ourselves. You must shift your mental paradigm if you want to migrate a dream to a place of reality.

I recall listening to the late Dr. Myles Munroe discuss the power of dreams and he likened dreams that are never fully birthed to being stillborn. See, failure to let go of the past robs you of the ability to commandeer the future. And when life is lived in the past, it is not life at all. It is just a kinda life or what I call an "if" kind of life, and I came to a place in my life where I determined that I could not live on "if" when real life was calling me.

APRIL 4, 2005

On that night, April 4, 2005, I vowed to become a new man. I sought to live a life dedicated to reaching my fullest potential. As I sat in my room on the night I was to be reborn, I wanted to live from a place of the spirit and not from a place of my fleshly desires. What I realized was that to do that, I had to find the warrior within me. I had to become reborn through dedicating myself to a life of self-discipline and focus intently on developing self-mastery and skill-mastery. See, self-mastery is required to obtain a level of occupational mastery. Mark Divine, the author of *The Way of the Seal*, stated that if one lacks dedication to developing self-mastery, it does not matter how good or theoretical their approach to self-leadership is. He believes it is character that determines performance. When you think about the idea of renewal or going through a state of change, you are really re-engineering your whole person. What I have found to be so true about Mark's statement is that to become a better version of yourself requires re-defining one's mental DNA; it is a stage of rebirth or renewal, or as I call it, renovatio.

I remember looking up the word rebirth in Webster's Dictionary. Webster defined it like this:

rebirth

1. a new or second birth: the rebirth of the soul.
2. a renewed existence, activity, or growth; renaissance or revival

I then looked up the word renewal because I realized at that point that I wanted to be more, I wanted to do more, and I wanted to achieve more. I knew that the man I was had to die and a new person would have to emerge. See, change happens when you get fed up. It only starts to happen when you get sick of being stuck and telling yourself you are powerless. You are never powerless; you are just not aware of how very powerful you are. Similarly, you are never truly a victim. You are only the victim when you think that you are. The difference between a victor and a victim is all about attitude. It is not the situation that is the issue; it is how you interpret what you are experiencing that determines the reality of it and that has everything to do with one's mindset. What had to change for me was not the odds but my mindset; only then could I obtain a higher level of performance and become the warrior I knew that I could be.

On that day I began to wake up to my own personal power. On that day I laid down my life, I got down on my knees and prayed for strength to become more than an average man. I wanted to be a warrior. I remember praying for the courage of David, the wisdom of Solomon, and the strength of Samson. It is interesting how we seek a higher power when we are in times of distress and we feel we are completely helpless.

Now, I was no stranger to feeling powerless or helpless. In fact, I started life off in a state of physical powerlessness. It wasn't my fault; it was just the way it was. I have little recollection of my early childhood. However, I know that I began life poor. I remember stealing food and hiding in the closet to eat it. I remember the first time I saw a cupboard full of food and being in awe that so much food existed in a home. In fact, I was told by my adopted mother that when she took me in, I had on a ripped-up t-shirt and little girls' underwear. Now the point of my story is not to make you feel sorry for me, but to help you to understand why I needed to renew my mind. I spent much of my life overcoming the past and trying to perform in the present. I lived life and I looked pretty normal, but inside I was dying. I spent many years holding on to the past. I did not know how to let it die. Sometimes you can keep moving, you can even keep ignoring, but eventually the past will catch up with you; and if you are living in the past, your whole person will eventually stop growing and potential will wither away.

So on April 4th, 2005 I decided to face myself. I decided that I had to slay my personal dragons. I had to make peace with the past and accept that I possessed a bright, beautiful future. It was that night that I woke up to my divine purpose.

That night I prayed because I realized that I could not overcome myself alone. Believe however you want to, but I believe that God listened to my prayer that night, and the miracle was not instant but gradually my spirit changed over time. When you appeal to your spiritual nature, you are able move mountains in your life. Prayer is powerful.

Now each person is unique in their beliefs on the topic of spirituality; however, spirituality is indispensable and it is linked to happiness in both children and adults. What I prayed for was a renewed mind. I had experienced many ups and downs from birth to the ripe age of 26 and I was ready to rewrite my story. Everyone has a story, but very few of us realize we can rewrite the outcome of our story. The battles are mental and spiritual but few understand that because they only operate in the physical.

What always needs constant renewal is your mindset. There comes a time in every person's life that they must humble themselves in order to help themselves.

I had to admit that humility was an area I was lacking in, but it was because I was compensating for my feelings of inadequacy. You know, I felt like I didn't quite measure up and I had a fixed idea about intelligence. Specifically, my own intelligence. I guess I did not feel smart enough or good enough. But I know now that I suffered from irrational thinking and it clouded my mind. So what is your mind set on? Remember this: mindset is everything. A weak mindset will keep you from heroic dreams.

PART 1

PURPOSE – OBSCURITY

CHAPTER 1

BECOMING A HERO

"Though much is taken, much abides; and though
We are not now that strength which in old days
Moved earth and heaven, that which we are, we are;
One equal temper of heroic hearts,
Made weak by time and fate, but strong in will
To strive, to seek, to find, and not to yield."
—ALFRED TENNYSON

A hero is defined and identified in many ways. A hero is defined as "a mythological or legendary figure, often of divine descent, endowed with great strength or ability; an illustrious warrior; a man or woman admired for his or her achievements and noble qualities; or one who shows great courage." To become a hero one must first become a warrior. Since the dawn of civilization, humanity has engaged in war and bred a class of elite fighters that were warriors. Some of these warriors became heroes and heroines. But before these average men and women were heroes, they had to become warriors first. Because a hero is defined as being a warrior, it is fitting to explore the warrior concept. It is a universally understood concept that is found in almost every culture throughout the world. The hero and warrior concepts are archetypes. An archetype is a universal symbol that is known unconsciously and is identifiable across cultures. In effect, archetypes are a familiar unconscious knowing or understanding of a certain, object, symbol, person, place, or thing that embodies who one is or wishes s/he could be. This archetypical figure is identified as a hero or heroine in stories where the hero or heroine sets out on a hero's journey to gain clarity and create balance in their lives. This warrior possesses specific characteristics that are required for them to navigate successfully in life.

Bruce Lee stated that "the successful warrior is the average man with laser-like focus."

Now, you and I were not born heroes, but we do have the capacity to become warriors and heroes. This is not just delegated to a fighting class. See, every one of us possesses the potential for greatness, but it is built on a foundation. The core foundation of discipline, preparation, and self-mastery are character traits that are embodied not only in these mythical stories of legendary heroes. These very traits reside inside of you too. In fact, they are essential to your achieving an elite level of personal work/life performance, they are important for you to become an optimal work/life athlete, and these are requirements to realize the better version of yourself.

What I have come to realize as I have grown older is that self-discipline is the main ingredient of success. Perhaps that was what was so appealing about the stories of my childhood. The power of the stories was that they gave me hope that if I worked harder, if I dreamed bigger, and if I developed my gifts, I too could become more than an average man. Isn't that what we all want? We want to be fearless in the face of our foes, we want to slay the giants that arise in our lives, and ultimately, we want to walk into the sunset knowing that we have overcome an insurmountable challenge. I have always loved the quote in the movie "Superman" where Jor-El, the father of Superman, stated:

> *"Earth's sun is younger and brighter than ours was. Your cells have drunk in its radiation, strengthening your muscles, your skin, your senses. Earth's gravity is weaker yet its atmosphere is more nourishing. You've grown stronger here than I ever could've imagined. The only way to know how strong is to keep testing your limits. You will give the people an ideal to strive towards. They will race behind you, they will stumble, and they will fall. But in time, they will join you in the sun, Kal. In time, you will help them accomplish wonders."*

Now I know we are not Superman, but we all have the potential to become more than just average men and women. We may not be fictional heroes, but we can become heroic in how we choose to live our lives. See, like you, I used to read myths, tales, and legends. My imagination would run free. I would find myself as the hero in stories like *Don Quixote, King Arthur, Lord of the Rings,* and *The Lion, The Witch, and The Wardrobe.* What was powerful for me was that these myths possessed gems of truth and they taught me lessons about valor, being victorious even when life presents the greatest of tragedies; and some stories and lessons helped me peer into the dark corners of myself. Carl Jung would call that your shadow self but we can just call that the beast inside. What I loved about these stories was that they told of good and evil and the redemptive qualities of forgiveness, the power of one more time, and learning from failure. What you learn from myths, legends, and stories is that finding truth is essential to finding one's potential, and potential begins with knowing and believing in yourself. What you learn from myths, legends, and stories is that the hero of the story is supposed to face trials. The stories I read also taught me that challenges are expected; inevitably, there will be a battle of some sorts. In fact, not every battle is won on the first try; some battles are fought over days and some over years. Sometimes you are meant to be temporarily defeated. The problem is not defeat; it is when you fail to learn about yourself in the process. You win some and you lose some, but combined together, these lessons teach you how to win in the long run.

This makes me think about the story of the turtle and the hare. I used to believe that life was all about speed. I had to be the fastest, I had to be the smartest, and I had to be the most cunning. But I have come to learn that it is less about quickness and more about being steady.

Every story starts out slowly and it is crucial that you are quiet, because as I learned as a boy, it is important to be quiet and listen for the lesson. In these stories I saw that the hero is always seeking to overcome something within himself or herself. The real fight we face is always within us. You cannot overcome or go to the next stage of growth until you have mastered the level before it. This is how the journey goes and this is how the warrior grows into the hero. And so every great man or woman walks his or her own path, whether knowingly or not. That is why you must understand that you are the hero of your story but I am narrating.

Now, let me tell you this, it will do no good to you if you spend your time seeking to replicate someone else's success or trying to adopt their vision. If you do this, you will never become the warrior you were meant to be and you will never begin the journey, because you have a unique purpose and when it is ignored, you are left under-fulfilled.

See, the law of purpose is that a unique purpose is given to each individual for them to utilize and serve the world with it. For instance, I love the story of King Arthur because Arthur was the one to whom Excalibur belonged. It was only he who could pull the sword from the stone. This is how purpose works. Your chosen purpose is yours to carry and not someone else's. You have to walk toward it and not from it and that requires commitment to a particular path, because your purpose is your burden to carry; it is your journey. So, it is time you begin to take the road to renovatio, i.e. the journey of the hero. Now let me explain this hero's journey for you or what I call it, which is the road to renovatio.

To be clear, the road to renovatio or self-renewal is really a road to achieving ultimate mastery over one's life. Ultimate mastery is arrived at by developing self-mastery in conjunction with skill mastery. But to obtain this kind of mastery requires understanding your purpose, knowing your gifts, overcoming your fears, engaging in life with the view of it being your work, learning from your experiences, and being deliberate about personal and professional development. Skill mastery and self-mastery require you to live with intention focused on continuous improvement and expectation. You must be committed to changing yourself. This is not an easy road to take but with intention, expectation, and practice you can become the better version of yourself.

Set an intention for yourself. An intention is simply a verbal action pertaining to what you will achieve or who you will become:

1. Identify something you value or a right action you are seeking.
2. Get up daily and "tell yourself" your day will be great regardless of any obstacles that may arise.

3. Now set an expectation for yourself. According to Andrew Newberg, the author of "How God Changes Your Brain," having an expectation about your goal is essential to achieving it. An expectation tells the mind that the goal can be reached.

So, who do you want to become?

THE HERO'S JOURNEY

Before we can become anything in life, one must first commit to something or someone bigger than themselves; this means finding something into which we can engage our full energies. For the average person to become the warrior, you must first commit to the narrow path of warriorship. I call it the road to renovatio; only then can the hero's journey begin. The Hero's Journey is based on the research of Joseph Campbell and his book, *The Hero with a Thousand Faces*. Campbell spent years studying mythology and stories, and what he learned was that every story is loomed with a common thread. The similarities in story and myth transcended race, culture, geographic location, and even time. Campbell's research found that every story, legend, fable, or "monomyth" follows stages common to every story ever told and is unconsciously known by everyone.

While I am not a huge fan of Campbell's views on faith, I do find his mapping of the hero's journey to be informative. I can see the phase I am in within my personal hero's journey. We really are living out a story. Each moment unfolds a new twist and turn on our lives. Unfortunately, some of us never seem to record the journey from start to finish. If this doesn't make sense, just think about King Arthur; the stories about him were based on a real king. What can be determined is that every story has a beginning and an ending, and every story revolves around some aspect of someone or something, and begins with a choice and ends with a resolution. It is through the articulation of a story that we begin to find ourselves; it is through the reading of someone else's narrative that we reflect on what life means to us; it is through a story that we begin to identify the character we personify in our lives; and it is through a story that we begin to understand who we are not, because it is through a story we are able to design the life, the character, and the path we want to take in our own lives.

A story can inspire you to act, it can inspire you to love, but the problem with a story is when you get stuck in someone else's story and you never begin writing your own. Now don't get me wrong, we begin in obscurity and we leave life with some form of a legacy, but very few of us consciously live life intentionally. We come into this world unwritten and leave the scrawled words of our souls on the memories of everyone that has entered our path. Ultimately, the beauty of a story is that it plants seeds of belief within us. See, your story and my story are the basis for the seeds of belief because it is through story that you and I learn that anything is possible. It is my intention to show you that what you want in your life is indeed possible. In fact, it was through reading the life of Viktor Frankl that I began to understand the importance of attitude in dealing with trials. Through reading the Bible I learned about salvation and redemption; through reading about the life of Nelson Mandela I learned about indomitable will; and through the story of the life of Miyamoto Musashi I began to learn the importance of strategy and the way of the warrior.

The truth is that your life is a story and you have the power to write a new vision for the future. So it is important that you begin to view your life as a narrative; it is a story, a book that must have all the pages filled before the end is truly to be written. Through the articulation of my story, you will learn the principles I learned when I began to take my own personal renovatio. The writer Maya Angelou stated that, "There is no greater burden than carrying an untold story."

For you the story begins when you decide to take the path of the warrior (the journey to become a hero). So, ask yourself if you have begun to take the step toward your dream and if you are prepared to take that dream and make it a written life vision, because all life is a story but it is particularly important that you begin writing yours down. Whether you write it down or not, your actions will be remembered and they will live on long after you are gone. So make it good! You don't have much time.

If you have not started moving toward your dream, recognize that your mountain is waiting but time is not waiting on you. Time is not on your side and it cannot and will not wait for you; and like every great warrior before you, you must come to the realization that while the greatest of warriors can become a hero, even he or she can never cheat death. In the end, the story concludes the same for the average man, the great man, and the hero; and that is that death is inevitable, so accept it and get on with living. The point is, a warrior must come to accept that one day he or she will die; this is very important so that they can savor the gift of this life and stop wasting time.

So, where are you? At what stage are you in your life? Have you begun recording your story?

Campbell identifies the hero's journey as a cycle. You will be surprised to know that most screenwriters utilize this model to make modern day movies. What is fascinating is that it actually replicates the life of an individual who possesses a desire to improve life performance; and I promise you that if you identify yourself as the character or the hero, you will know exactly what stage of the story you are in and how it relates to your life right now. So, review the hero's journey and tell me where you fit in on the path. You are on a path whether you choose to acknowledge that or not.

RENOVATIO INTERPRETATION OF THE HERO'S JOURNEY

- **Ordinary World:** You are living an ordinary average life. You are average and do not know your potential.
- **Call to Adventure:** You are faced with a crisis that requires you to ignore or assimilate to a new mindset. At this point you are hoping, but you do not have the faith required to move you forward.

- **Refusal of the Call:** You refuse to accept that you need to make a change in your life because of a fear of discomfort, fear of change, because you feel alone, or untrained.
- **Meeting with the Mentor:** In order to prepare for the journey, you need a coach to prepare you mentally for the struggles ahead.
- **Crossing the First Threshold:** You begin to walk with courageous fear forward toward the adventure.
- **Tests, Allies, Enemies:** You are learning how to operate and maneuver in your work and life. You are learning the rules of engagement. Your will is being tested by trials of endurance and tests of strength and will. At this time are you surrounding yourself with individuals that support your cause? Are you aware of those who don't want to see you succeed? You will experience both and it is important that you recognize both.
- **Approach:** Setbacks occur. At this stage you may believe you have achieved personal mastery and skill mastery, but you possess a fixed mindset until you experience something that will get you unstuck.
- **Ordeal:** Your mindset is changed by a major event that tests you and you overcome it.
- **Reward:** Upon overcoming this major milestone, you realize you have great potential but you have not perfected your person. You still have a ways to go. You have finally tested your skills but this is just practice.
- **The Road Back:** After the minor ordeal, you begin to go back to a life of familiarity but you are unaware of the life challenge ahead. This challenge is what is to take you to the level of mastery.
- **Resurrection Hero:** You are now at the stage where you accept your whole self and you know your full potential. You understand your personal power and you know how to use your giftedness. Now you must use everything you know and have

learned to face the greatest battle of your life. Every moment flows into this moment, right here, right now.

- **Return with Elixir:** You have overcome your great challenge and it is your job to transfer those skills onto the next generation or be a mentor to someone else, because you have been where they are going. It is your calling to now be the fuel to light the God-given flame of their talents, so that they too can find their way.

So where are you on your walk?

While you may see yourself in the hero's journey and find it to be a concept that you already know, while it may sound familiar to you, the question is where you are on your journey. For many of you, it is likely at a place of obscurity. Are you willing to commit to the path of the warrior? Are you willing to take the road to renovatio? Because the path is an uncommon path only taken by men and women seeking to realize and harness the potential that lies within them. So, what is the hero's journey you ask? How is it described? And where are you on it?

To understand the journey of a hero, it is important that you understand that (1) every hero must first become a warrior, (2) every warrior takes the path of warriorship and (3) this path of warriorship is what I call the road to renovatio, or road to self-renewal, and it is a path to wholeness, and it begins now.

THE WARRIOR ARCHETYPE

The warrior, like the hero is viewed as an archetype. An archetype is a universal symbol that is known unconsciously and is identifiable across cultures. In effect, archetypes are a familiar unconscious knowing or understanding of a certain, object, symbol, person, place, or thing that embodies who one is or wishes they could be. You could argue that the warrior archetype was the first form of an athlete. In fact, warriors have existed as long as man has known the art of war. See, a warrior is a brave or experienced soldier or fighter. According to Robert Spencer, the warrior ideology "comes from the type of discipline and focusing used by ancient warriors to prepare for battle. To maximize the chances of surviving, the warrior led a disciplined life that required self-mastery and a way of being in the world that was beyond what ordinary people could manage. It is the tradition of discipline, preparation, and self-mastery that forms the core of the modern warrior myth". In her book *Archetypes*, Caroline Myss says the warrior archetype is representative of physical and emotional strength. This warrior archetype has the ability to protect and defend himself or herself. Yet, the warrior utilizes weapons of the mind as the first weapon of choice. The warrior's goal is not to harm the opponent unless all other options are lost. Physical confrontation is the last resort.

What is important is that you understand that the warrior I speak of fights a battle to overcome the "self" and wrestles every day to renew mind, body, and spirit, and check his or her emotional state. This warrior wages war with his/her mind in order to develop an immovable mind that is continually on target. The warrior I speak of is what I call the renovatio meaning-based warrior. They continually renew their minds, they are aware of their mental, physical, and spiritual needs, and strive to reach a level of self-mastery in order to achieve skill mastery.

This warrior I speak about is an elite work/life athlete who optimizes every experience to be the best version of his/herself. The warrior is a symbol of hope and discipline. Even when everything is shaken around them, the warrior is unshaken within. The warrior I speak of cannot be broken because the power of the renovatio meaning-based warrior is the power of the spirit. It is through spiritual renewal and the continuous quest to seek guidance from above that endows the warrior with the will to meaning, and it is this pursuit that takes the average person from ordinary to extraordinary. See, a man or woman is not born a warrior; s/he must seek to become one through the development of their whole person.

The biblical book of Joshua identifies the importance of being immovable or unfettered. Joshua was a warrior before he was ever a leader. He was told to be steadfast and to not fear. King David was told to be fearless and not fear. Carlos Casteneda states:

> *"To be a warrior is not a simple matter of wishing to be one. It is rather an endless struggle that will go on to the very last moment of our lives. Nobody is born a warrior, in exactly the same way that nobody is born an average man. We make ourselves into one or the other."*

To become a warrior is a path that begins now! It begins in every minute and every second of your life. To become a warrior requires finding a direction because warriorship is a path that requires a vision. While it can be likened to leadership, the difference between the two is that a warrior must first learn to lead him or herself before they can lead another. While the average person seeks to lead through the wielding of external power and outward influence, a warrior focuses on developing their personal power; it is the power of self-control or self-management or self-will that defines the warrior and allows this person to lead from the inside out. Similarly, a warrior seeks a vision because the warrior understands that meaning in life is a spiritual journey, requiring it to be viewed from the mind's eye and not the natural eye. His life is his work and his work is to identify the true purpose of his life. The path the warrior takes is the path of spirit.

See, it is within that all courage, all fear, all success, and all failure take root, and it is within that you must go to uproot limiting beliefs that keep you from performing optimally. This can only be done by acknowledging that there is a need to strengthen the mind, body, and more specifically the spirit. You must become a triple threat!

In the book *Compassionate Samurai* by Brian Klemmer, he stresses the importance of connecting to the spiritual aspect of yourself because it is the biggest aspect of who you are. He refers to the spirit, body, and soul as a three-part snowman and your spirit being the biggest component. In his view, the spirit is essential to being a compassionate samurai and is essential to achieving peak performance. In fact, achieving peak performance or optimal performance is a process that entails seeking the vision of your life through the art of envisioning. Envisioning is a creative process which when it gets down to it, is a spiritual endeavor. All creativity comes from inspiration and inspiration means to be inspired or inspirited.

What is your vision for your life? If you do not have a vision, how can you optimize your performance?
Dr. Myles Munroe states, "Remember that sight is the ability to see things as they are, and vision is the ability to see things as they could be." I like to go a step further and define vision this way: vision is the ability to see things as they *should* be, and that is why the warrior leads from the inside out, because the real battle is the battle to overcome himself. You must learn to see the places within you because that is the place where the real enemy lies. The real enemy to freedom is fear. The real enemy to your vision is the shortsightedness of fear.

The Renovatio Meaning-Based Warrior is a warrior that leads from the inside out and fights from within. To become more than an average man, a man must see beyond his present in order to be and become the future that lies before him or her. The reality is that what is sought to make you great is inside of you. For the average worker and the average citizen, this desire to be right-aligned with one's self is screaming out to them but they continue to muffle its cries. The warrior continually seeks purpose, self-understanding, self-mastery, and harmony in work and in life. Warriors continually seek the vision and accept that the true cause he is living for is the cause within. Their vision is to become more than average men and women. They seek to be fully self-actualized. Their vision is to be directed by a higher purpose and to live by a higher law. Vision will take you farther than your natural eyes can see. The truth is, your eyes are not fully open and you cannot see because you are searching for all that is in you, but you are looking in the wrong place. Meaning is inside of you, purpose is inside of you, and it is going to take everything you have got within you to allow the warrior within you to reflect on the outside of you. But first you must stop looking with your natural eyes and begin looking with your spiritual eyes. Bruce Lee believed in the importance of developing the inner spirit of the warrior. He understood that this force was vital for living an optimal life and it was the key to achieving optimal performance. In his book, *Striking Thoughts*, he alluded to the all encompassing nature of the spiritual force when he stated:

> *"For as long as I can remember, I feel I have had this great creative and spiritual force within me that is greater than faith, greater than ambition, greater than confidence, greater than determination, greater than vision. It is all these combined. My brain becomes magnetized with this dominating force which I hold in my hand."*

What you seek to bring out of you is the inner man/or woman; that is what you have caged inside of you. All your true potentials lie dormant. It is time to find the warrior within you. You must find him if you are to attain the vision for your work and life. Welcome to the road to renovatio or self-renewal. It is time to PUSH yourself to a higher level

17

of human performance! Perhaps you should not pray for an easy life but for the strength to endure a difficult one, as Bruce Lee advised.

Every great performance requires a high level of endurance. It is not how fast you go that matters in life but how long you last. So, it is essential that you train to optimize your time and run your race with diligence until the clock stops ticking. The clock is ticking. You better get running. Now, are you ready to PUSH?

COACHING COMPONENTS

THE WARRIOR WHEEL & PUSH MODEL

The warrior wheel contains the PUSH model. The wheel represents the connection between the internal and external need for competency development. The PUSH model is a cognitive model, meaning it is focused on transforming your mental processes through internal investigation and inquiry. It boosts executive functioning of the mind and teaches the coachee to develop metacognitive functioning. The focus of the model is to develop self-mastery and skill mastery.

WHAT IS MASTERY?

Miyamoto Musashi, a 16th-17th century Japanese samurai, ink painting artist and author of the classic strategy text *The Book of Five Rings*, would tell you that mastery is something you will never truly arrive at. Be it self-mastery or skill mastery, both are a requirement to achieve greatness. Self-mastery is the process of learning to discipline your mind, body and emotions, so that you can achieve skill-mastery or a high level of competence in a field. These are relational concepts. For instance, when a coachee comes to me, they are typically impacted by a performance issue. But upon uncovering their issue, it becomes quite clear that personal issues are impeding their ability to perform a skill or task required to achieve a goal. Typically it is mental, emotional, or simply a lack of understanding about a task or situation.

It is in my opinion that one must develop the ability to PUSH themselves daily:

- Know their **purpose** or their why for living life and do what they do and keep them on their personal road to renovatio.

- Continue to get and acquire **self-understanding** through daily assessments and practicing mindful activities, such as journaling.
- Work daily toward **self-mastery** – this requires not only tuning in and being aware of themselves but also working on both their personal strengths and weaknesses. This comes in the form of building mental toughness and will building for resilience.
- Work to keep their life in **harmony or in balance** – this requires them working on all areas of themselves mentally, physical, and spiritually in order to stay right-aligned.

WHAT IS SKILL MASTERY?

Much like self-mastery is a daily process of personal development, skill-mastery is about reaching one's full potential in their given field; and to do this requires understanding that skill-mastery is really a lifelong process of development.

In fact, the two work in tandem. Research in the field of expertise development describes the process as a lifelong journey. In order to become an expert or be elite, i.e. or to be great, it requires understanding:

- **Motive**- refers to understanding your mental or psychological state or orientation to learning a skill, art, or task.
- **Competence** – the system of practicing which involves knowing what is required to be successful. These are the skills required or techniques needed to improve upon a skill.

- **Reason** – having a compelling reason or understanding of why you are trying to achieve through constant self-analysis and self-assessment. Understanding the reason for your efforts.

But more importantly, it is important that you recognize that it is a whole system process. That means all aspects of you must be working together to achieve "Arête" or virtue; that's basically the highest good. Researchers Young Koung Moon, Eung Jung Kim, and Yeong-Mahn detail this system as the development of your:

- **Self-system** – refers to the motive or mental motivation for wanting to learn a skill. This must come from within you.
- **Practice System** - when you possess an understanding of what the skills are that are required to make you great.
- **Meta System** – this is a system of inquiry or questioning that is required to help you analyze and determine how to make your performance better. This is when you focus on continuous analysis of your performance to understand how to excel at something.

It is key that you recognize that the development of personal and professional mastery form the foundation for life success. Do not believe that genetics determine greatness. Rather, hard work is what makes the difference. Ultimately you have to p.u.s.h yourself.

I obtained the name PUSH from listening to an old coach named Coach Kerner. He was my high school track coach. Kerner used to tell us that we had to P.U.S.H. I liked the term, but he used it as a general term.

For the renovatio meaning-based warrior, it is an acronym and it is pretty powerful when used to transform the average person into a bonafide beast! I can still hear him telling me, "Michael, you have got to PUSH," but the acronym for the P.U.S.H. assists you to:

- Identify **purpose** – Why are you here, what do you want?
- Increase **understanding** – Why do I do what I do, and is what I am doing directing me toward purpose?
- Improve **self-mastery** – What do I need to master within myself to achieve a level of control over my destiny?
- In order to arrive at a state of **harmony** or well-being – Am I working to keep myself in balance as I seek to achieve this vision for my life?

I have found that these are essential components of coaching clients and optimizing performance. In fact, many individuals I coach lack an understanding of their unique purpose because they do not possess the self-understanding required to improve self-mastery or skill-mastery and so they can not arrive at a state of harmony. They cannot actualize their full potentials because they have never really sat down and asked the essential question: what is my purpose in life? Believe it or not, purpose is the beginning of identity and awakens the potential that lies within you. When you find purpose, you can direct your life and optimize every minute of it to become the better version of yourself.

Another thing that is important for you to understand about my coaching is that Renovatio Meaning-Based Warrior Coaching revolves around understanding your trajectory. The trajectory of the Renovatio Meaning-Based Warrior focuses on the stages required to develop greatness, i.e., elite performance. In order to do this, the renovatio meaning-based warrior follows a warrior trajectory that revolves around developing the inner person. This focus on inner work improves purpose, self-understanding, self-mastery, and harmony or well-being. The Warrior trajectory is identified by four stages of development and is focused on developing skill-mastery and it is grounded in learning theories and human performance coaching. A warrior begins in a place of:

IDENTIFY VISION	IDENTIFY YOUR FEARS	LEARN HOW TO USE YOUR GIFTS	ENGAGE IN DELIBERATE PRACTICE

4

MASTERY

3

AWARENESS

2

TRUTH

1

OBSCURITY

1 — OBSCURITY

No one knows who you are. You are dreaming about being great. You are contemplating greatness. You are not sure how to achieve it. You don't know what you are capable of yet. You know you want to be more, do more, and achieve something more. You start to identify who you want to become. You begin to craft a vision. You identify your purpose.

2 — TRUTH

You begin the process of identifying who you are at your core. You are seeking to uncover the truth about yourself. You begin to identify your personal beliefs, values, and you get honest about your strengths, weaknesses, fears, and gifts. You identify what is holding you back from greatness. You become clear about what you want and what you need to do to achieve the vision using your talents.

3 — AWARENESS

You develop awareness by exposing yourself to challenging situations. You find avenues to test your mind, body, & spirit. You engage in self-reflective practices. These practices develop mental toughness, self-knowledge, and reinforce confidence and belief that you can become the better version of yourself. You begin taking action toward your goals.

4 — MASTERY

You recognize you can be great but you must:

1. Focus on deliberate practice by getting a coach or mentor.
2. Commit your life to the development of self-mastery in order to achieve expertise.
3. You learn to overcome your mind to create the reality you want.
4. You develop SMART goals and focus on directing your thoughts and rewiring your brain.
5. You develop mastery over your brain through mental force to achieve your goals.
6. You stay focused until you have become the better version of yourself.

1. **Obscurity**

   (P) Identification of Purpose. In the stage of obscurity, warriors are not warriors yet. They are seeking to identify themselves. At this stage, they are in a state of polarity. What they are experiencing is the desire to pursue a calling but not sure of themselves, nor are they sure of their potential. Their potential is unknown, so they reside in a place of obscurity.

2. **Truth**

   (U) Development of Understanding is required in this stage. But to find truth, one must first be honest about who one is, overcome what is holding one back, and set a vision for what one wants to be. At this stage the warrior contemplates taking the path to warriorship. Through a process of self-analysis and questioning, the individual determines what they are able to excel at and what they are passionate about, and with this truth they can direct their energies toward a purpose. This is the beginning of making a commitment to achieve "arête" or rare excellence.

3. **Awareness**

   (S) Awareness and development of Self-Mastery. In this stage, warriors become committed to the path of Renovatio and seek to renew their thinking by acting and living out their vision for their lives. They become committed to the path of Renovatio, or the hero's journey. At this stage the talents of the warrior have been realized, actualized, but it must be honed from continuous improvement. It requires developing personal power over the self. Warriors then begin to direct their meaning toward a purposeful pursuit because they are aware of who they are, what they want, and they have seen what they are capable of.

4. **Skill Mastery**

   (H) Harmony through the alignment of the mind, body, and spirit. Through aligning their gifts and abilities with work and life pursuits that focus on legacy building, warriors walk a path to higher performance and attain ultimate mastery. They have learned to go beyond their preconceived notions of their capabilities. At this point, they create rather than copy and leave a legacy behind in the process. But it is also at this point that they realize they can never truly attain mastery or perfection because it is an illusion. They realize that they are boundless and they are meant to never stop going beyond. You must learn to become limitless in your thinking. To become limitless requires mentorship. You must become a mentored mind.

CHAPTER 2

A MENTORED MIND

*"No man is capable of self-improvement if
he sees no other model but himself."*
—CONRADO I. GENEROSO

As you know, all warriors destined to be heroes are given mentors along the path that teach them lessons and help them to hone their mental and physical skills. These lessons are imparted and aren't always impactful at the time of hearing them, but over time they are recalled. Many times we don't interpret the lessons because of a lack of experience, the time is not right, or we are not ready to receive the power of the message. But if you remember anything, know that the seeds of truth are like a tree, and when they land on good soil, they will slowly grow with you. I didn't come up with that; Jesus did. In any event, it is essential to find a mentor when you begin taking the path to spiritual renewal and ultimate mastery.

The ability to achieve high levels of performance mastery is best achieved when the practice is deliberate and it is done with a coach or a mentor. K. Anders Ericsson, an expert in the field of expertise emphasizes the importance of engaging in deliberate practice. Deliberate practice is a form of practice that focuses on developing a specific area of development. Typically, it is an area of weakness that needs work. While the average person wants to avoid criticism, the high performer seeks to understand and be critiqued on what they are not doing right. The significance of this is that to arrive at a level of mastery requires the utilization of a coach. Ericsson's book *Peak*, elaborates on the philosophy of deliberate practice. He identifies seven components required for one to achieve expert performance.

- You must practice a skill that already has tried and tested techniques and this must be done with a coach who understands experts that have attained expertise in the field of practice.
- The practice must push you beyond your comfort zone.
- Your practice must be specific and focused.
- You must engage in the activity with your whole self.
- You must seek to understand how to improve a given skill by engaging in self-correcting behaviors. Get feedback and adjust accordingly.
- You must understand how activity should look and adjust your technique to make sure it mimics the correct way of doing an activity.
- You must learn to build on the fundamentals that you have learned.

Mentorship and coaching have been the staple of the warrior for centuries. In fact, this is a common process when a man or woman is seeking to find his or her way. Cyrus the Great was tutored by Cambyses, his father. Cyrus states that his love for humanity, courage, and wisdom were due to the lessons he learned from his father Cambyses. He noted that his father taught him, "to endure labors and undergo dangers for the sake of heroic achievement". What Cyrus understood from his father was that a man builds and leaves a legacy behind. But it was not physical wealth, it was the virtuousness of his character.

Because you and I will be remembered for something, and whatever we do in this life will either be praised at the end of our lives or it will be a cause of another man's sorrow, Cambyses taught Cyrus the importance of living with the end in mind and leaving beautiful memories. Now beauty, I believe, comes from a life that is lived for a purpose greater than you or me. Legacies are built on purpose and require daily practice to achieve expert performance.

LEARN HOW TO BUILD A LEGACY FROM CYRUS THE GREAT

Cyrus the Great wanted to be remembered for his achievements; he wanted what he accomplished to live on after himself. He hoped that the power of his presence would linger in the minds of his warriors and they would embody the virtues he upheld throughout his life. There are two things that can be learned about Cyrus the Great: While he was known for being a liberator of humanity, and while it was prophesied in the Bible before his birth that he would liberate the Jewish people, Cyrus developed expertise as a warrior because he was mentored by his father at an early age. He also sought to be virtuous in his actions.

See, virtues are merely values and beliefs that we adopt as our own. These values and beliefs are the drivers of our behavior and they determine the direction of our lives because they create our character. You likely developed a belief system and values from a parent, mentor, or friend. Regardless of how you acquired these values and beliefs, I guarantee that throughout your hero's journey, you have learned many lessons along the way. Because what is true about life is that it is full of lessons that one is taught and these lessons are what shape character. Character is who you are and it is instilled in you from a young age.

The ancient author Marcus Aurelius highlights the power of character and how behavioral modeling of a mentor influences our own personal greatness. In his book titled *Meditations*, he discusses his philosophy on life and identifies what character meant through the observation of his father Antoninus Pious. It was Antoninus Pious and social interactions with those around him that developed the virtues in Marcus Aurelius. It is important to live your life as both a participant and observer. In fact, Marcus Aurelius' book *Meditations* is a book of reminders that he wrote to himself about his philosophy on life. It was his modus operandi, or way of seeing the world; the way you see the world is based on what you believe, what you fear, and what you value.

For me, I had to ask myself how much of what I believed was because I was conditioned and taught to believe that way; I had to ask myself if I believed in God because I was taught to or because I knew in my heart of hearts that He was real and had a unique purpose for my life. Now I have come to know my beliefs and have continually worked on my character. Am I flawed? Yes, but what warrior or great hero is not? Was Cyrus a flawed man? Of course, but it is important for you to understand that Cyrus the Great's view of the world was based on what he gathered from his personal experiences and the lessons learned from his mentor. I believe they spent much of their waking hours listening for lessons in each moment. They likely spent more time learning than trying to teach. In fact, if you analyze these great men, what you will notice is that they were always learning through the observation of themselves and of those around them.

They learned by modeling the behaviors of others that they held in high esteem. The psychologist Albert Bandura coined this as "social learning theory" but the relevance of this is that one can learn or adopt behaviors based on whom they observe. See, you can learn to be moral, aggressive, or good from a person whom you hold in high esteem; you learn and model what you see on TV and what you read. So, it is important that you:

- Filter the things you read. To achieve great things, you must read the work of great men and women.
- Surround yourself with people smarter than you.

I have learned to filter what I see, what I hear, and with whom I associate. Because when you are seeking to grow, you cannot sit with the dead. You must surround yourself with what gives life and does not take it from you. So who influences you? With whom have you allied yourself? They will either support you in the remaking of yourself or they will faithfully tear you down. Please, choose wisely.

Now understand that some lessons may be good; they may be bad too, but they will educate you and teach you how to deal with the ebb and flow of your own life because they are teaching moments. Many times you are not taught all the lessons by only one teacher, but your character is determined by how you deal with difficult situations in your life.

So, if you seek to take a new direction in life, you must find someone already on a similar path to greatness. It is critical that you find a mentor who can inspire you to rise above and push beyond what you think is possible, and possess good character, and make sure they are true to their trade. You must align yourself with someone who embodies more than the ideal of success, because real success is living authentically, placing your faith in God, and finding those who share the same sentiments as you.

To do this, I believe they must possess truth. Are you seeking truth or accepting every lie told to you? Yes, I have experienced this as well. That is why you must seek guidance from God; otherwise you will be led astray. Yes, I have been led astray by my own ideas about life. But eventually I realized I was foolish and needed a guide. The great warrior Miyamoto Musashi cautioned against taking the journey of life alone.

Miyamoto Musashi understood this point and taught his students about the power of truth. He stated that: "Truth is not what you want it to be, it is what it is, and you must bend to its power or live a lie." One thing I can tell you is that a fool ignores truth but a wise man accepts good counsel. This is why men and women of greatness sought to surround themselves with counselors who were seeking truth. Please, do not exchange truth for a lie, because in the end it will only lead to disappointment and disillusionment.

The reality of life is that many of us are living a lie instead of seeking to find our truth. Truth is the ultimate striving of the warrior. For the warrior, finding truth is essential to taking the path to renewal or renovatio. How can you become impeccable in work or life if you are not honest about your skill sets, what makes you happy, and ultimately what makes you unhappy? To not know your own truth means you are living a lie. To not know your truth is to forfeit real wealth, and it destroys any chance of you ever realizing what is truly valuable or meaningful in your life. True understanding comes from true exploring, searching, and authentic mentorship. Bruce Lee suggested that "one must challenge belief in order to arrive at truth." He further suggested that a belief is only true "if it can be acted upon without upsetting one's expectations".

I believe that he is right: you must challenge your beliefs and search for truth; but when you find truth, it is important that you take action toward changing yourself. You have to be hungry for truth; some of us say we are hungry for truth but eagerly eat the lies about us. Sometimes we can't move forward because we do not have a guide and sometimes we do not move forward because we would rather starve than accept that we don't have all the answers. Therefore, it is important that you choose the right teachers to help you on your spiritual journey. When Jesus set out on His ministry, He chose disciples who were hungry for truth. If you are hungry for truth, then it is inevitable that you will find it.

You prepare to change your direction when you come to a realization of who you really are. A mentor will show you truths about yourself but no one can make you change. Only you can do that.

The power of truth is that it allows for you to see the low-hanging fruit required for you to develop both personally and professionally. For instance, how many times have you been dishonest with yourself and your abilities? You know what I mean: someone explains something to you and you pretend as if you completely understand the complex topic presented, but the reality is you did not understand a word that was being said. Miyamoto Musashi stated this about individuals who appear to have arrived at truth. He suggested that one must understand the inner and the outer and to shy away from believing in one's own self-importance.

In fact, it was his belief that only through "constantly searching from within, based on one's lifestyle, can truth be known and this is a personal process."

Quite simply, true performance is arrived at when you understand yourself and your craft. To live otherwise is really just operating in a state of hubris. The Greeks identified hubris as an individual who possesses a personality of overconfidence that teeters on the side of pridefulness. Here is the truth about hubris: I was guilty of it, and because of it, I was not able to perform at my highest level. And I likely missed out on powerful teaching moments in my life. The warrior recognizes that being teachable is a prerequisite to becoming impeccable or achieving excellence. Are you teachable?

REMOVE YOUR EGO

In order to accept truth, you must remove ego or "hubris." One of the first stories I ever learned as a boy was the story of Icarus. You may know this story. Icarus had a father, a great inventor named Daedlus, who invented wings so that he and his son Icarus could escape a labyrinth. Icarus was instructed not to fly to high towards the sun because the wings were made of wax, and if he flew too high his wings would melt and he would fall to his death. Because of his overconfidence, he flew higher and higher toward the sun, not noticing that the wax was melting and he fell to his death; and that is an example of hubris. So again, are you teachable?

Accepting truth allows you to overcome your ego. Real growth and development cannot be achieved when you are not listening; it only occurs when you are seeking understanding. You must learn to listen for the lessons. I spend much of my time listening and seeking to understand the lessons I learn from my life performance outcomes. I have come to understand that comprehension is not mastery. What you must ask yourself is: are you teachable? The biggest issue with many of us is that we are not really teachable. We would rather die than explore the basics of our profession, or admit we do not know as much as we thought we did. But mastery attainment is the process of continual improvement. It does not offer room for ego or hubris. It only allows room for humility and learning. Similarly, it is important that you find a mentor or a coach to reach ultimate mastery.

GREAT WARRIORS WERE GREAT STUDENTS

It is just as important that you find a mentor who aspires to not only greatness but a firm foundation built on something spiritual; for me that is someone who does not doubt the power of the spirit, and realizes that the human experience requires understanding how to optimize the mind, soul, and sprit. If you read more about Cyrus, you will realize that Cyrus the Great possessed a strong moral compass. This is essential for becoming the better version of yourself. It is also essential that you do not become a copy of your mentor. They are merely a mirror to help you reflect back who you are. In my own life, I have found it necessary to find tutelage from more than one person. When you have access to more than one mentor and you are able to extract the good qualities of the various mentors in your life, it improves your self-knowledge, provides you with varying perspectives, and increases the speed of personal life mastery and task mastery. Robert Greene, the author of *Mastery*, suggests that to attain mastery requires becoming an apprentice, developing your skills, and experimenting with what you learn. Similarly, the great Samurai Miyamoto Musashi suggests not taking the path to self-mastery and skill mastery alone. Because it is a difficult road that few can navigate on their own.

MENTORSHIP IS IMPORTANT ON THE PATH

Now you likely have or will have many teachers who will come into your life for a moment to teach you something you need as you continue your journey or your personal road to renovatio. At some point, these mentors will leave when their time is done and they have served their purpose in your life. Each mentor teaches you a little more about the world around you and the potential within you. Some mentors will teach you the power of humility and you may have others who teach you a far more important lesson. The second-most important lesson is that they are imperfect men and women, they are flawed and are prone to mistakes just like you. They teach you who you do not want to be, just as they teach you who you are. You must learn to extract the good qualities from them but never become like them.

See, you are always being taught lessons by different mentors, even when they are not aware they are teaching you something. Simultaneously, we all are building our legacies. As you write your story, your mentor writes his or her story, because valuable information is always being shared. It is through mentorship or a quality coaching relationship that you will heighten your performance and learn expert secrets of how they have mastered their lives and their professions in order to rise to their desired goals in life.

Coaching and mentorship are the quickest ways to ultimate mastery. The reason is that a mentor can transfer knowledge they have learned over their lifespan that makes the road to developing ultimate mastery faster. I love to read about King Solomon. I spend much time seeking counsel from the Bible because it is a book of motivation, a book of mentorship, and it is a means to build character. But what Solomon suggests is that you seek wisdom even if you have to pay for it. "The beginning of wisdom is this: Get wisdom. Though it cost all you have, get understanding." I believe that it is important that you understand that reading and learning and knowledge are great, but what creates expert performance is when that knowledge becomes wisdom. Your greatest and quickest road to developing wisdom is through a mentor, teacher, or a more advanced life athlete, i.e., a warrior.

When you do find a mentor who is both knowledgeable and possesses wisdom, you must seek ways to apply the lessons you are learning to achieve the better version of yourself. In truth, the wise recognize that they are perpetual students, but the knowledgeable approach things with the belief that they are experts. You must be teachable. Are you teachable?

When you study individuals who have aspired to greatness, you will notice that they were mentored by someone, they were teachable, and they spent hours or years developing their craft. Alexander the Great was mentored by Aristotle, Martin Luther King, Jr. was influenced by Gandhi, Plato was mentored by Socrates. Paul of Tarsus was influenced by the mentorship of Barnabas, the Twelve Disciples were mentored by Jesus. What all these men came to understand was they had to always be awake and listen with discerning ears because greatness comes from listening for the lessons. Are you awake? Are you listening with discernment?

Lessons are typically learned through engaging in experiences. Now some lessons you take to heart right away. Some lessons just don't make any sense for you in the moment. These are those lessons that go deeper than just surface teaching. They are profound moments that possess a slow, gradual impact. They are like slow burning stars. Did you know that a star's lifespan is determined by its mass? The smaller the star, the more staying power it will have.

One thing I know is that it is not about the big bursts of energy that allow you to achieve your goals in life, but rather the small, slow-burning light that you cultivate within you that refuses to burn out. The smaller a star is, the longer its lifespan. Much like the star, some life lessons are seemingly small but they stay with us the longest. Perhaps it is the unobvious nature of the lesson, but over time the significance of the experience grows as you grow in maturity and understanding. Please realize that the simplest teachings and seemingly trivial experiences may have the greatest impact on your life direction, work pursuits, and path to self-renewal. Never take time extended to you for granted. Keep every lesson no matter how big or small safely guarded until the opportune time.

Some things you should discard. Bruce Lee suggested that one should only take what they need from life experiences and discard what is not essential. You must extract what is vital and discard what is not necessary for your life journey. Because if you carry more than you need, you will never reach the destination; it will either tire you out, or you will be weighed down. What I am getting at is that you may need to let go of the baggage that is keeping you from performing at the optimum level; you may need to go back and reassess the experiences in your life and find a way to embrace the good and the bad, but then you have to know when to let go of what is holding you back. So, have you identified what is holding you back? What is that thing that is causing you to burn out? I bet it's something in your past. Now there is nothing wrong with honoring the past but do not stay there; you must let go and always move forward!

What I am saying is that to optimize an experience is to look at it seeking understanding in it. You must gain self-knowledge from it, because every experience is meant for your successful journey. What you must do is learn to shift your perspective by listening for the lesson. This requires listening for the lesson in the story of your life. Otherwise you will never get on with the journey, and the objective of the journey is to grow into an unstoppable force powered by an unconquerable spirit that submits to the will of God. The power you have is the ability to reflect on your work/life experiences and listen for the lessons that come from living life. But it requires you to approach life with a beginner's mind.

How to find a mentor?

- Find someone in your profession or field that exhibits qualities that you want to emulate. Ensure they are reliable and possess a record of success.

- I asked for mentorship from someone I highly respected and knew that I could count on.

- Set a time to meet with them weekly, monthly, yearly, or as needed.

BEGINNER'S MIND

"When you're faced with looking at your own life with awkward eyes, you will have increased a bit in knowledge of yourself (in other words, your mental and physical abilities will become clear to you), and knowledge of anything outside of yourself is only superficial and very shallow. To put it another way, self-knowledge has a liberating quality."

— BRUCE LEE, STRIKING THOUGHTS

You must engage in your daily interactions with the mind of a child or with a beginner's mind, because interactions and experiences help us to understand ourselves. Even the smallest lesson is a means to help you navigate the direction of your life, and it will show you where your gifts are.

Now, some lessons are found in the most obscure places. These are lessons learned without even knowing they are lessons. I love how Jesus commanded this of His followers; He said, "Truly I tell you, unless you change and become like little children, you will never enter the kingdom of heaven." A child's mind is void of obstructions. They do not understand limitations and they are humble in their desire to know, learn, and grow.

If you observe a child, what makes them beautiful is that they are inquisitive, they do not easily get embarrassed, and they love life because for them life is play. The best scientists possess this childlike nature and that is why they discover new things. What a child will teach you is that you don't have to always be serious to be productive. In fact, learning through play is a powerful way to overcome mental barriers. They will show you how to see the world with new eyes. Perhaps this is their purpose in our lives. To help us see life realistically. A child listens for the lessons and they learn through play.

I have a friend named Jason who is an amazing mixed martial artist. He has three little girls. He plays with them, and in the act of playing, he teaches them to spar. They have no idea that they are learning to defend themselves, and the power of the lessons won't be understood until they are older. But the truth is they are learning self-mastery at a young age. One day he will reveal to them the purpose of the lessons.

Much of my lessons have been learned through trial and error because mentors do not last forever; my first mentor, my father, died when I was 18. But I have been blessed by other wise men who have come into my life. Their lessons live on in my mind. They are the lessons guarded for safekeeping. These are the lessons that you keep close to you. In fact, they are so close that you forget them until they are needed once more. See, some lessons are meant for a purpose, and that purpose is to help you understand the nature of your own existence; and sometimes they are meant to fuel the eternal fire of your will. Because one day, you will default to them when you know no other way.

These lessons stay small as flickers and they burn within you until it is time for them to be brought to the surface. They are what I call your eternal flame. You must rekindle this fire within you or find it, and that is how one becomes a warrior: by finding the buried courage and potential that lies within him or her. This is acquired through living a life of mindfulness where you listen for the lesson. To find them is going to require you to listen for the lessons that are taught to you. You must be slow to speak and eager to hear. So, let's begin at the beginning. I want to tell you about one of my first lessons. It was something beautiful. It was the beginning of my desire to find my purpose in life. Listen for the lesson so you can p.u.s.h. forward in life.

How to cultivate the beginner's mind

A powerful example of this is Kano Jigoro, the father of the martial art "Judo." Legend has it he told his students when he died to "bury him in his white belt." While he was considered to be a master black belt, he always wanted to be viewed as a perpetual student. Think deeply on this.

Do not focus your mind on the outcome of a situation or event. Focus only on what you can learn from the situation. An open mind seeks only to learn. Command your mind to focus on what the experience can teach you. Tell yourself that it is not about winning or losing, only learning.

What area of your work or life can you approach with a beginner's mind?

CHAPTER 3

A LESSON
ON STARS

"Every man should lose a battle in his youth,
so he does not lose a war when he is old."
— GEORGE R.R. MARTIN

As a child, my father would pull out his telescope and impart fatherly wisdom about the infiniteness of the cosmos. One night he told me about the nature of a star. He described in non-scientific terms that a star was a hodgepodge of gases and matter forced together by energy for the purpose of lighting the sky through an internal eruption of energy that radiates externally to produce a noticeable glimmer, glow, or light for all to see.

My father was not a scientist, but he explained to me that the source of the light radiated from within this mass of gas and heat. I thought to myself that people are like stars: always shining and always in the process of being and becoming, and life is a fluid, continuous race that requires starts, stops, conscious pacing, and mad dashes where we push to a foreseeable end. Although we are engaged in our life, we see no end to it. But like every man and woman before us, we face existential questions that force us to open up about the finite nature of our lives. You know, the age-old questions: "What is my purpose in life? Why am I here? Is my work making a difference? And what is my potential? Because I don't know if I am living up to it."

These deep musings are aligned with your human motivations, human design, and they determine the direction of your life. In fact, they define the magnitude of your performance and are the reason some persist at things longer than others.

PURPOSE ACCORDING TO FRANKL

I did not know it then, but what I pondered as a boy were questions of my existence. Such inquiries pertain to personal significance and they have everything to do with optimizing work/life performance and ultimate life fulfillment. They form the basis for finding meaning in your life as you seek to fulfill your life's purpose or endeavor to find the purpose for your life. Of course, these questions require a great deal of personal thought, but they are part of becoming a warrior who takes the path of warriorship, or as I call it the road to Renovatio, or the path of self-renewal and spiritual awakening that is sometimes called the journey of the hero. Each one of us either avoids or welcomes these ultimate questions; and no matter what, at the end of our lives, we must revisit them. So, my philosophy is that one must seek to answer the questions now before it is too late.

The existential psychologist Viktor Frankl stated that man possesses an innate desire to give as much meaning as possible to one's life, to actualize as many values as possible, which is called "The Will to Meaning".

Frankl contextualized meaning as being derived from logotherapy. Logos is intended to signify "the spiritual" and beyond that, "the meaning".

What that means is the act of living a meaningful life, the act of performing life at optimal levels, is more than physical. It is a spiritual endeavor.

WHAT DOES SPIRITUAL MEAN?

Spirituality is an overarching concept that does not necessarily mean one is religious. Honestly, it means different things for different people. However, it is a driver of the human experience that can best be summed up as the spiritual aspect of every human being. Each one of us has a spiritual nature, and we all seek a meaning or reason to live, work, and perform. But Spirituality as a whole can be summed up as the search for a sense of meaning, purpose, and morally fulfilling relations with oneself, other people, the universe, and experiences in a collective sense, according to Edward Canada.

The reality is that meaning is an intrinsic experience that is spiritually driven. Because it is spiritual in nature, your inability to find meaning or purpose and your inability to achieve higher levels of human performance are not a result of anything outside of you; it is driven by something inside of you that is not being adequately developed or even ignited in the first place. You must learn to be fully engaged by developing the whole person, i.e., the integration and alignment of spirit, soul, and body. The need for integration is essential to developing the whole person. This was what I was missing in my life. But we will get to that later.

Oh yeah, whole person development is indispensable for creating well-being. Well-being really just refers to you as a person being healthy or fully alive. Abraham Maslow would have called this a fully actualized person, meaning a person who is able to unleash and engage in life using their full potential. In fact, well-being relates to performance because it is driven by the engagement of your whole self in the act of work and just plain old life.

So, do you engage your physical resources, your mental resources, and your spiritual nature in the work that you do and the life that you live? The problem with the average person is that they only engage their body and souls but neglect to improve the spiritual aspect of themselves, and this keeps them basic or average. Consequently, full development does not occur. Being fully developed means continuing to learn, grow, and develop your gifts and talents, because life optimization is the ability to engage body, soul, and spirit for the purpose of achieving a goal or end. What is important for you to understand is that you are divided in three. Your person encompasses Spirit, Body, and Soul.

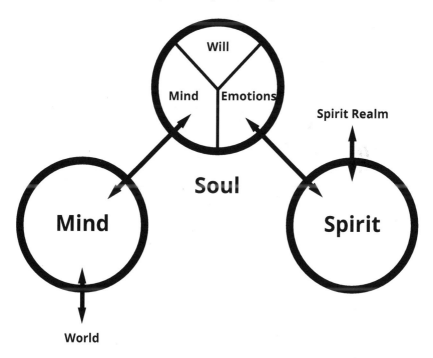

- **The human spirit** gives us a consciousness of self and other remarkable, though limited, "God-like" qualities. The human spirit includes our intellect, emotions, fears, passions, and creativity. It is this spirit that provides us the unique ability to comprehend and understand and it's how we connect with God.

- **The soul** is the immaterial part of a person from which flow their actions, thoughts, desires, reasoning, etc. It is separate from the physical body. It is the part of the person that makes a person what he is: alive, aware, able, etc. It is the essence of personhood; it is consciousness.
- **The body.** How we relate to the things around us through our senses of sight, sound, smell, taste, and touch. It is also called the outward man and inward man.

WHAT IS THE INWARD?

The inward man is the spiritual nature of man. It is where the true potentials are awakened. It is the immaterial or metaphysical. The metaphysical cannot be seen with the natural eyes; it is heavily driven by a mindset of belief and faith. We are spiritual beings. The inward man is the spiritual aspect of who you are.

WHAT IS THE OUTWARD?

The outward man is the fleshly nature. This is the aspect of men that focuses on the pursuit of material or the physical nature. We are sentient beings. We are matter, sensation, perception, mental formations and consciousness. The warrior is always in conflict with the inward self and the outward self, which is a daily battle.

The difference between the average man and the warrior is that the average man appeals to his carnal or sensual desire, while the warrior relishes in the comfort of self-mastery in order to overcome impulsiveness.

What is important to understand is that mastery requires all of you to achieve it. To develop mastery over a task or skill requires leveraging all aspects of yourself. This is what it means to be whole-souled. It means to be fully involved in the act of living, acting, being, and becoming. What is remarkable about human nature is that to experience one's full engagement, to arrive at a state of flow (which is a form of engagement), one must be aligned body, soul, and spirit in an activity. In their book *The Power of Full Engagement*, James Loehr and Tony Schwartz describe the process of becoming fully engaged as being contingent on our ability to manage the vitality (life force) or energy that encompasses mental, physical, spiritual, and emotional energy; they believe all are important and essential to growth and performance and must be in balance or harmony. I would have to say I agree. So, are you wondering how you tap your potential?

EXERTING YOUR WHOLE SELF

Exertion is a requirement to catapult you to a state of higher awareness and performance because pressure unleashes the gifts within you. Maslow calls these Peak Experiences because in these times you experience a heightened state of awareness. The author of *Flow*, Mihaly Csikszentmihalyi, would call it a flow state, which is a state of enjoyment that comes from exerting one's self or pushing one's limits. In sports it is called peak performance "or being in the zone," and in the field of work it is called work engagement.

But what all this really means is that human beings by nature are designed to perform at optimal levels of functioning, but few of us ever actually extend our reach beyond a point that may make us uncomfortable. It also means that we are designed to work with passion, live with passion, love with passion, and worship from a place of passion. So, perhaps being engaged in work one enjoys is more important than the work one does.

What I have come to learn in stories of old is that individuals engaged in the process of preparing for their unique purpose, and identified their gifts and talents, which they found through being mindful of their gifts. More importantly, those who became warriors and heroes always wanted something more. They never wanted to just be basic. In fact, they worked whole-souled to become more than average. They simply set in their minds that they could not and would not be average. In *The Pursuit of Excellence*, Ted Engstrom relates the importance of not being average. He stated that above-average individuals know how to balance their energies; they learn to be self-managed because they know how to manage their wholeselves. In fact, being above-average or realizing greatness requires going above and beyond the basic impulses and learning to develop your higher order thinking capabilities. Remaining basic really relates to using your lower level mental faculties. See, the brain is divided into three sections:

THREE BRAINS

Name	Location	Function
Brain Three Outside Surface wrapped around Brain Two Neocortex, also known as the coping brain. Newest brain.	Sits on top of the limbic system "neocortex"	It regulates our thoughts, reasoning, problem solving, and regulates our emotions & impulsivity. This brain is more reflective and introspective.

Name	Location	Function
Brain Two Wrapped around Brain One "limbic system" Second oldest.	It wraps around the reptilian brain.	Regulates our emotion. Such as joy, rage, fear, pleasure and pain.
Brain One Center of the Brain "R complex" reptilian brain Oldest brain.	Located in the middle of the brain. It is at the center. It focuses on survival.	Regulates desire for hunger, food, shelter, sex.

Your lower-level functions and drives focus around survival needs. The basic drives for food, shelter, hunger, sex, etc. Your second-level function is the limbic system that regulates your feelings and emotions, such as fear. Of course, there is nothing wrong with any of these drives, but when they dominate your life and divert you from your goals, they become problematic. Similarly, the limbic brain is not bad, but as an emotional regulator, it is opposed to pain and only seeks pleasure. It is averse to painful experiences and only wants to feel good. Which means that it is important to learn to regulate instinct and desires by using the logical aspect of yourself, and that is through the problem solving and coping mechanisms of the neocortex. So, are you seeking to be basic or are you seeking the better version of yourself?

If you find yourself:

- Constantly seeking pleasure
- Constantly avoiding pain
- Always overcome by emotions

- Thinking and obsessing over a desire or need to fulfill hunger, security, safety, etc.
- Living in problems
- Very impulsive

This means you have a low level of mastery over your emotions and instincts and you have not fully integrated the spiritual aspect of yourself. The truth is most people live between brain one and brain two, whereas I want you to operate with better control over your whole brain by effectively using your neocortex. Because the neocortex is where your creative thinking, problem solving, and self-awareness functions are available and when trained it can override the instinctive and emotional brain. Why, you ask? Because this is important to living and performing life at optimal levels.

WHAT IS OPTIMAL?

Being or living at an optimal level means to experience life being the best you can be; it is living up to your potential. This requires overcoming yourself by taking back control of your brain. The Navy SEALs, monks, and athletes train to overcome themselves. They do this so that they can perform at their best, even in the direst of situations. Warriorship is merely a focus on developing self-mastery and skill mastery so that you can optimize your human capabilities and live life more self-directed instead of being directed by others. Great performance comes from great practice. But what is really being trained is one's capability to manage the mental hardwiring in your brain. If you can manage the mental game, you can overcome the obstacles in front of you. Remember: the battle begins in the mind.

Jeffrey Schwartz and Rebecca Gladding, the authors of *You Are Not Your Brain*, suggest that there is a difference between your mind and your brain. You can alter your mind, and when you do so, you rewire your brain by focusing on changing your mind. You have the power to filter and interpret moments, events, and situations. When you reconstruct your reality, your brain responds to situations according to what you tell it and not according to how it feels.

Oftentimes I run with my clients. Why? Because running hurts and it sucks for them. But in the process of running, they face the challenge of mastering their mind, their physical bodies, and the desire to quit. Running is a natural way to experience both pleasure and pain. The biggest thing your mind and body tell you when you are running is that you are tired and this hurts when you are exerting yourself, which requires you to know your body, know when pain is deceptive, and know when you need to reframe your mindset. What you begin to realize just from running is that:

1. Your body will experience pain, but it is not really pain; it's just being pushed harder than usual.
2. Your mind will tell you it's tired when it is not.
3. A little voice in your head will say this is boring and maybe you should stop.

GET OUT OF YOUR FEELINGS

Many times, we don't succeed because we live life based on how we feel at the moment. We lose focus because we feel like things are not how we want them to be. We live from that emotional brain. But here is the thing about that emotional brain: when you live life based on how you feel, you can't get anything done.

As an entrepreneur, if you consistently don't feel like making calls, as an athlete if you consistently don't feel like training, as a worker if you don't feel like going to work and you consistently appeal to the side of your emotions... the outcomes will be disastrous. You will never achieve a higher level of performance. Maybe you need to get out of your feelings because when you make decisions based on feelings or emotions, they inhibit you from optimizing your full abilities because feelings and emotions do not necessarily represent truth. For instance, the SEALs focus on the 40 percent rule. This basically means that when you believe that you are done with a specific effort, you still have more left in you to give. Have a 40% rule; your mind gives out at 40% effort, but your body still has 60% more it can go. This really suggests that what you think you can do and what you can actually achieve should never revolve around your feelings or emotions. Maybe that is why so few of us ever reach a state of self-actualization and even fewer people crack the code of their true potential. Remember: your emotional brain is averse to pain and only seeks pleasure.

How To Get Out Of Those Feelings

Taken from Jeffrey Schwartz and Rebecca Gladding, the authors of You Are Not Your Brain

Step 1: Relabel. Identify the deceptive brain messages (i.e., the unhelpful thoughts, urges, desires and impulses) and the uncomfortable sensations; call them what they really are.

Step 2: Reattribute. Change your perception of the importance of the deceptive brain messages; say why these thoughts, urges, and impulses keep bothering you (it's not ME, it's just the BRAIN!).

Step 3: Refocus. Direct your attention toward an activity or mental process that is wholesome and productive - even while the false and deceptive urges, thoughts, impulses, and sensations are still present and bothering you..

Step 4: Revalue. Clearly see the thoughts, urges, and impulses for what they are: sensations caused by deceptive brain messages that are not true and that have little to no value.

Now, when we talk about optimal levels, we are really focusing on moving beyond just living for the basic needs and pleasure. To be optimal means to think and operate at your highest level of consciousness. It means to live with an elite mindset and not be basic. You were never meant to be basic. You were meant to be unstoppable, renewed, and immoveable! So, understanding performance, and more importantly optimizing your performance, will allow you to live an extremely productive life. That was what I wanted to do when I started my personal renovatio. I wanted to perform well in life and find happiness, but I was too young to understand what optimal performance meant to me.

Like most kids, I lived in the space between instincts and pleasure and wasn't all that logical; I was and continue to be very high strung and high energy. That was until I found running. I loved and love running because it allows me to feel free; it forces me to run outside of my comfort zone. See, you can run for miles but no matter what, you must remember that at some point, you will have to run the other way.

I have learned to never worry about the length of the run because that is not what is important. What is important is what

I think, do, and feel while on the run. But the real reason I love running and sports is that they teach you how to self-regulate your instinctive nature, your emotions, and your logic, and they allow me to go beyond myself; and oftentimes I run and pray. See, as a young runner, we were taught to listen to our bodies, become aware of our emotions, control our breathing, and will ourselves forward in a race, even when our bodies were tired. We were taught to give everything of ourselves, leave it all on the track, and we learned to push through our pain because we learned that pain was necessary; it was honorable to throw up during a workout because that meant you pushed your body to its breaking point, but it also meant your ability to tolerate pain increased. When you exerted yourself beyond your normal capabilities, it only made you stronger. It willed you further, and in the end, it gave you a sense of euphoria but what the runner learns is that greatness is earned, greatness is learned, and to achieve it requires embracing the path to it. It is definitely a metaphor for life.

Ray Lewis talks about pain and the importance of learning to embrace pain in order to experience the other side of pain, and that is that triumph is the expression of greatness in human form. We fall short of realizing the other side of pain because many of us give into our emotional brain and this aspect of ourselves is averse to pain; it just doesn't want to struggle. But the truth is that pain is a necessary evil in life if you seek to grow into something more powerful; it is necessary if you want to become the better version of yourself.

What I know is this: that you must embrace pain and learn to find pleasure in discipline. We learned this at an early age. If you know anything about running, one of the hardest types of training you will ever do are intervals. These are speed work exercises. We used to run through hills, forest preserves, often rising early. We learned to strengthen our will, but we didn't know that was what we were doing because we found ways to enjoy the moment, we reveled in the wins, and we knew no limits because we spent our waking hours overcoming our physical and mental barriers. We were simply playing, experimenting with our abilities; all the while we did not know we had found the secret formula to success in life, and it was called "practice." Maybe it doesn't make you a perfect person, but it does allow you to achieve a perfect effort.

Here is the truth: practice is painful when you view it as practice, but when you see it as play, it becomes enjoyment. The funny thing about running is it taught me a lot about life and it is the default I have always gone to when things have gotten hard. When I found out my father died, I ran. Before I got married, I ran. Running has been my solace since I discovered it in elementary school. But the point of this story is not to tell you about running. It is to tell you to listen for the lesson. See, it is the lessons from my youth that were the basis for who I am today. If you read about Nelson Mandela, what you will learn from his autobiography is that he loved to box, and he excelled in sports. In fact, it was his knowledge and understanding of strength conditioning that kept him sane during his decades of imprisonment on Robbin Island. Mandela developed a regiment of daily exercise that consisted of running, push-ups, sit-ups, and boxing. All of which were practices or rituals that he developed in his youth and utilized throughout his life. What are your rituals? Do you have any? Because these will keep you when the going gets tough and you can bet it will.

How to Develop Daily Rituals

To develop a daily routine requires identifying what you do on a daily basis that makes you feel powerful. A habit is unconscious but a ritual is consciously done. Here is what you can do to develop daily rituals.

1. Keep a log of your daily activities to determine which routines are helpful and which are harmful.
2. Ask yourself "what do I do during my day that gives me energy and or empowers me?"
3. Determine what you do in your day that is disempowering or takes energy from you. What are those things? List them.
4. Commit to the rituals that are beneficial to your vision for your life and improve your performance.
5. Schedule these activities as "must do's" and write down why it is necessary for you to do them on a daily basis.

DISCIPLINE YOURSELF

At the age of 19, Mandela found he loved the disciplining nature of sports and he utilized this to strengthen himself and lessen his level of stress. What Mandela was doing was building his coping ability, and the mechanism for coping with stress comes from the rational brain. In fact, James Loehr and Tony Schwartz explain that experiencing tension in our lives is a requirement for growth and development. They suggest that it is important to building all areas of our lives and essential to improving our mental, physical, spiritual, and emotional components of ourselves. Now I did not know all of this as a child, but as I reflect on life now, I realize that from a young age I focused on developing my whole self, and that this was necessary for me to overcome my greatest obstacle in my life: me. The great battle you face in your youth and in your overall life is your ability to overcome what you have been through to become who you are supposed to be. Discipline allows you to embrace the struggle and move forward against all odds because you become fueled by your own fire.

One thing I can say is that I always had an eternal fire burning within me, and like you, I would express that fire in self-destructive ways. You know, lacking control over my emotions, being easily upset, and blaming the world. In a way, you could say I wanted to tear down instead of build-up. But it was because I did not have a healthy outlet for my pain. See, sometimes that eternal fire cannot be contained and when this occurs, it burns you up inside. Have you found a way to manage your emotions? Running was the way for me to unleash all that potential in me. It allowed me to overcome my force of nature by unleashing it through competitive play. It allowed me to focus, reflect, and aspire to always be better. It taught me to reach for the stars because, as I found out so long ago, that is where greatness lies. Greatness lies out of reach until you stretch your hand out and move toward it. I do not believe you can truly experience greatness when the past is holding you back. A warrior learns to let go of the past to focus on his or her future.

What I mean is that at first what you want may seem like a far-off vision, but it isn't. It is merely positioned in a place that will require you to stretch yourself in order to grasp it.

Write down your personal vision. Identify what you want to be, do, feel, think, associate with, and impact by some date in the future.

Use the following questions to craft your vision.

Based on your personal experiences, what do you find joy in doing every day?

My greatest strengths/abilities/traits/things I do best:

At least two things I can start doing/do more often that use my strengths and bring me joy:

Now, in 50 words or less, write your personal vision statement:

Here is my personal vision statement as an example for you to use:

"My vision is to develop mastery over my mind, body, and spirit so that I can teach and educate my clients to develop mastery over their work and lives in order for them to achieve optimal functioning for optimal performance in both work and life."

Note: You may want more time to think about your vision. Don't ignore this. Learn more about why it is important by reading pg. 154.

CHAPTER 4

BACK TO THE LESSON ON STARS

"I'm a dreamer. I have to dream and reach for the stars,
and if I miss a star then I grab a handful of clouds."
—MIKE TYSON

Your know, as I look back on the lesson of that starry night, I remember that there were so many stars in the sky that my tiny little hands could not reach them but still I tried. I focused on just being there; in that moment I saw the glimmer and glow and nothing else mattered. It seemed like when you are a child, you are more motivated to explore your potential. I attribute this to the power of our innate and natural tendency as children to possess a beginner's mind. In Thomas Sterner's book called *The Practicing Mind*, he talks about this concept and describes it as a time when you are completely absorbed in an activity. That absorption keeps you focused; and depending on what you do, focus is important, because if you turn your eyes away for a second, you could get hurt. A beginner's mind is a mind that approaches every challenge and every opportunity as if it is a first-time experience. This is important because when something feels new, you possess no limits; in fact, you possess no real understanding of a situation, and so you focus in on the situation or circumstance in order to understand the nature of it. But when you approach a situation with new eyes, new understanding arises.

- So how do you approach your work or your life? How do you approach challenges?
- Do you limit yourself by living with a limited vision and clouded mind? This only limits your ability to produce the results you seek.
- When was the last time you observed your place in the world and decided to reach out for something more?

When you choose not to reach for that something more, you train your mind to avert growth. Stop limiting yourself.

WHY ARE YOU LIMITING YOURSELF?

What I do not understand is why so many of us limit our minds; we limit the possibility of what we can do because we focus on what we believe we cannot do. In fact, it is such a commonality with most people because our minds are biologically geared toward negative bias. That means it already believes that it is incapable, and that is what it will tell you. You know what I mean: that little voice in your head that always tells you that you are not good enough, you are not talented enough, and you can't achieve it. Not to mention your critical fans. These are the people who pretend to root for you, but they secretly want you to quit or fail, and then you have the ones who will tell you outright that you will never make it. I have experienced them all, but I have found that the worst critic is that inner voice inside of you. That is why you need to learn to master yourself.

If you want to combat the negative thoughts, begin by focusing on truth. What I mean is this: most times the things you tell yourself are not really true at all. So it is best that you:

- Denounce these thoughts as lies.
- Engage in positive self-talk.
- Identify daily the things you have been blessed with or you have achieved.

But whatever you do, stop lying to yourself! You are stronger than you even know.

GREATNESS IS NOT LIMITED BY TIME OR SPACE

Now you may think that it was foolish for me to think that I could even touch the sky or grab just one star. Perhaps you are right, but great ideas are born from inspiration and great performance comes from a deep belief in one's ability, and more importantly placing faith in Almighty God and tapping into creative abilities. Remember this: nothing is impossible until it is done and that is what makes the great, great. They approach their performance with purpose and that purpose is to continually improve. A warrior approaches each day with new eyes; they dream big, but they recognize that it is going to take daily efforts to achieve optimal performance. You must begin each day with a new mindset and that means renewing your mind.

- Pray
- Meditate
- Exercise
- Read something inspirational.

What you were yesterday does not determine the outcomes of today. Your performance yesterday does not determine the success of your today and this must be the way you think, day in and day out. Most importantly, without faith you cannot achieve greatness because:

- Developing a talent or gift is hard work.
- Mastery may take years for it to be realized.
- You will never arrive. You will continually become better but never arrive.

If you are an entrepreneur or a person experiencing a time of transition, then you must understand that faith is a prerequisite. Without it, you will quit before you realize the extent of your abilities because:

- Expert performance takes time to cultivate.
- To optimize your talents is a lifelong journey.
- Mastery is an illusion meant to drive you to be the best version of yourself.

WHAT MAKES GREATNESS?

Now, greatness is a topic that has been studied for centuries. The research began with the work of Sir Francis Galton, who argued that people vary hugely in "natural ability," which he believed was inherited biologically. Galton was the cousin of Charles Darwin, and he believed that genetics were the basis for elite performance.

Current research on the topic of greatness is more specifically focused on talent and giftedness. Research in the field of elite performance identifies achievement as being based more on one's ability to practice. K. Anders Erickson has done research in the field of performance and found that deliberate practice is what is required to become the top in one's field. Now the truth I believe is that greatness and rising to an elite level of performance are attributed to many different variables: time spent at a task, the discipline of the individual, the amount of support, the identification of others that one possesses talent, and personal tenacity required to keep going when everything inside of you says turn left and everyone around you says quit. I think that greatness is a combination of so many variables, but the most important thing you need to realize when it comes to greatness is what greatness means to you and what it looks like in your own life. The only way to seek greatness is to ask yourself who you want to become and work toward cultivating your gifts and talents to arrive at your vision for your life.

HOW DO YOU DEFINE GREATNESS?

I define greatness as the ability to fully optimize one's mental, physical, and spiritual potential while being present during moment-to-moment life events, in order to achieve a higher purpose or calling. In the field of sports psychology, it is well known that optimal performance can only be attained through whole person development. According to Patricia S. Miller & Gretchen A. Kerr, the authors of *Conceptualizing Excellence: Past, Present, and Future*, it is only "through full development of the individual that optimal performance can be attained". Every one of us seeks to attain an optimum level of performance, but why is it that so many of us never arrive at our full potential?

The reality is that to achieve an optimal state of performance requires developing an inner state of awareness through personal development and inner mastery. Unfortunately, we don't live our lives the way we are designed. We are designed to experience full engagement in our lives. We are designed to develop our whole selves, we are designed with the drive for higher motivations, and we are designed to serve a higher purpose. When we are able to tap into our potentials, we are able to achieve greatness in life.

WHERE DOES GREATNESS COME FROM?

Greatness comes from legacy-building activities and not pleasure-seeking. Legacy-building activities are usually the things you do that give meaning to your life and the lives of others. They are purposeful activities. Every time you act on behalf of another and expend your energies and your talents for someone else, then you are acting heroically and living purposefully. Similarly, when you have served someone else at the expense of yourself, this is what is remembered when a person thinks of heroism. See, warriors become heroes because they served someone else with little regard for themselves.

They became heroes because they chose to hold on longer than anyone else. Those are the moments when your greatest struggle becomes the catalyst for life's greatest changes.

You know what I mean? These are those meaningful moments in life when you and I give of ourselves, expecting nothing in return – not even a thank you – because we simply did what we were born to do. You could call this warriorship, you could even call it heroism, but at the end of the day it is all these things and it represents what you value; it is who you really are because a warrior is someone who is not afraid to express freedom of choice or free will. You have the freedom to create the life you want. Warriors understand this, and it allows them to recognize that they possess a will to meaning. This will to meaning is the understanding that you are free to achieve goals and purposes, because as a spiritual individual, your life is yours to shape. Viktor Frankl stated, "Human freedom is not a freedom from but freedom to". We all recognize we have a freedom from, but very rarely do we exercise the freedom to:

- Rise above your current life circumstances.
- Change the direction of your life.
- Be reborn into a stronger, more courageous self.
- Take our own unique path in life.
- Work and live on our own terms.

Here is the truth: you have both a freedom and responsibility to live your life with a purpose. If you are looking for happiness in your life, stop looking for happiness and begin by engaging in meaningful activities that create meaningful experiences or optimal experiences that lead to more well-being in your life. I believe that in the 21st century, happiness is confused with hedonism or the seeking of pleasure. Why do we have this belief that a life void of struggle is happiness? Why do we not understand that anything worth having requires hard work, sacrifice, and lots of faith?

In fact, the reality is that the most rewarding experiences in our lives come from the greatest of struggles and these are typically regarded as the most meaningful moments in our lives.

Mihaly Csikszentmihalyi suggests that the most meaningful experiences are the ones that force you to stretch yourself. These are the experiences that cause you to reach deeper inside of yourself. He refers to them as phases in our life where we engage in a struggle to conquer a trial. These are what he calls optimal experiences, which are essential to personal and professional development. In fact, he states that:

> *"When people try to achieve happiness on their own, without the support of a faith, they usually seek to maximize pleasures that are either biologically programmed in their genes or are out as attractive by the society in which they live. Wealth, power, and sex become the chief goals that give direction to their strivings. But the quality of life cannot be improved this way".*

Therefore, it is important that you realize that happiness and the quality of your life are enhanced by your willingness to engage in work and meaningful activities that cause you to stretch yourself. Realistically this is the opposite of how most individuals live and operate in life. But it is the reason for the high levels of discontentment and under-fulfillment in people's lives. The reality of life is this:

- We simply do not want to accept that goal attainment requires a certain level of goal striving, i.e. "struggle."
- We don't understand what creates lasting happiness. We are obsessed with short-term gains over long-term success because we do not know how to differentiate between pleasure and purpose.

ARRIVING AT GREATNESS REQUIRES FOREGOING PLEASURE

In his book, *The Iron Will*, Orison Swett Marden would identify great men and women as having an iron will, which he described as being able do what one plans. We call this willpower, which is the ability to delay immediate gratification. For centuries this has been man's greatest adversary. Man versus his impulse. When I speak about being basic, what I am saying is that our impulsive and instinctive natures must be disciplined in order for us to achieve a goal. In the Bible, the Apostle Paul tells us to run the race with a purpose and he even tells us to beat our bodies into submission.

In retrospect, when we are unable to control ourselves, we become more like beasts. Being instinctive and using intuition are important to developing mastery but what differentiates humanity from the beast is our ability to self-reflect and reason. We spend much of our lives either being in command of our nature or being commanded by it. Now later, I will talk about asceticism and its relationship to modern athletics. Well, the premise for warriorship, athletics, and goal attainment are all the same. One must master themselves in order to achieve mastery over a skill.

When you are not in control of your human nature, it becomes a force of nature that destroys everyone and everything around you. That is why it is important to develop self-mastery so that you can attain a high level of work/life mastery.

MASLOW'S HIGHER NEEDS OF HUMAN NATURE

Of course, to truly understand human performance, it is important that you understand that true human performance is the ability to achieve optimal performance. This is really another way of expressing the innate need to grow and develop or improve your well-being. When you seek to experience increased performance in work and or life, it is really another way of expressing your higher needs, or what Maslow calls your higher motivations. Human nature is driven to go beyond basic desires. What we all want is to transcend the mundane and continuously be more, do more, and achieve more. Because all performance is driven by motivations, it is essential that you learn to go beyond being basic. See, being basic is only living for your basic human drives; but if that is all you are living for, what separates you from the animals?

The philosopher Aristotle defines the difference as our capability for rationality, reason capabilities, and virtue – or in Greek, "arête." This relates to performing well in the act of being human. In his view, perfecting a skill and being really good at something allows you to find happiness in your overall life. He also believed that being virtuous was important to leading a successful life. The point I am making is that skill acquisition is not the summon bonum, but it is one way to make life more meaningful; in fact, it is another word for "work" because to work and work well requires practice.

Now, don't get me wrong: we all need to fulfill the basic drives for food, money, and shelter. This is our instinct for survival. But the warrior learns to go beyond these basic desires because the warrior understands that staying basic does not equate to living a life of significance. To the contrary, when you allow yourself to stay stuck and do not continually develop yourself through the process of self-development, you stunt your growth and deny your potential to achieve ultimate mastery. Understand that when you stop growing yourself, you will slowly wither away, because that is when you will stop knowing yourself.

WHAT YOU NEED TO DO TO ATTAIN ULTIMATE MASTERY

Life-mastery is about designing the life you want by basing your work and life around who you are at your core. What many people experience in life, and this is likely you, is dissonance, a state when your behaviors do not align with your values. It is when you lack the ability to be true to who you really are because you live contradictory to what you believe. I believe it is time you get right-aligned with yourself. Ultimately, to achieve your idea of success, you must develop personal mastery, i.e. self-mastery and skill mastery. But you cannot do that if you are not right-aligned with your values and beliefs and behaviors. Are you experiencing dissonance in your life?

You will know it because your actions will conflict with your values and beliefs. So, to fix this, it either requires changing your beliefs or changing your actions so that they work in harmony.

Here is the bottom-line: you must learn to master yourself before you can master anything else. Leonardo Davinci stated it best when he said:

> *"You will never have a greater or lesser dominion than that over yourself... the height of a man's success is gauged by his self-mastery; the depth of his failure by his self-abandonment... and this law is the expression of eternal justice. He who cannot establish dominion over himself will have no dominion over others."*
>
> **— LEONARDO DA VINCI**

At the heart of greatness is a life of improvement and the willingness to learn to be impeccable. Because what a lack of self-development indicates is that you lack the mastery over yourself to achieve a desired end. What we call that is getting in your own way. When you are unable to differentiate between a want and a need, when you lack the willpower to overcome something, someone, or yourself, you actually fight against your innate need to actualize your full potentials, and this ultimately derails you from living a purposeful life because you do not live in the moment. Rather, you waste energy on just trying to survive. Survival can never lead to actualizing your potentials because actualizing your potentials requires you to feed your body, soul, and spirit. Every part of you is essential to the success of you. Why? Because you were designed that way.

HUMAN DESIGN

Aristotle described human beings as being teleological by nature, which means you are designed to fulfill a unique purpose or calling in life. The purpose of your human design is to move beyond the need for safety, food, and shelter. You must get beyond being basic in order to experience growth needs or your higher human needs, such as the cognitive need of meaning, aesthetic needs such as experiencing beauty, self-actualizing (or the need to learn and grow), and the need for self-transcendence, which is experienced through the service of another or the worship of something bigger than you like God. Human beings are designed to live from the inside out and not the outside in. When you seek to understand your unique purpose, and identify your God-given gifts, you are aligning yourself with your unique and natural human design. You must live from the inside out if you want to grow and develop in achieving both work and life mastery. When you are able to align them, what you achieve is ultimate mastery. For the warrior, achieving an ultimate state of mastery is the way to achieve balance.

SO, WHAT DOES THAT MEAN?

What this means is that you can make your life meaningful by pursuing your gifts and talents. The problem for so many of us is we don't seek to understand who we are, and we give up when things get too hard, so we never truly develop the potentials within us. If arête is believed to be the greatest or highest good, then human performance and the development of talents are aspects of arriving at some level of happiness in life. The problem with most individuals is that they do not have the power to stay with something long enough to see it realized. We simply don't cultivate the power of our will to see our visions through, and that is because we don't always know the difference between pleasure and purpose. See, pleasure is fleeting but purpose is life-transforming. In fact, the difference between pleasure and purpose is an area I did not understand for a long time. But I will share that with you.

When we seek pleasure in an activity, it is really meant to endow us with a feeling of happiness or feeling of fulfillment and meaning. This is what Aristotle termed Eudomania, i.e. well-being. What most of us engage in are mere hedonistic pursuits. Hedonism, which is common in our society, focuses on gratifying physical desires through fleeting external pleasures. What Aristotle realized is that lasting pleasure comes from activities or pursuits that will give your life real satisfaction, but these experiences are typically long-term endeavors.

What is believed to create psychological well-being or happiness are (according to Carol Ryff):

Self-acceptance	Accepting yourself for who you are
Positive relations	Building quality relationships
Autonomy	Having the freedom to think, act, and live on your own terms.
Environmental Mastery	Possessing a feeling of control over your environment.
Purpose in life	Pursuing meaningful goals and finding purpose in life.
Personal Growth	A continued pursuit of personal growth and excellence.

SO, HOW DO YOU APPROACH YOUR WORK-LIFE EXPERIENCE?

You can find meaning in work and meaning in life, but it needs to be relevant work and related to your overall life purpose to improve your ability to learn, grow, and develop yourself. If your work lacks these components or the activities you engage in are lacking any of these areas, then you are likely in need of a transition. Because unfulfilling pursuits only waste your life and warriors do not live life to waste time, because time is a precious commodity. That means that you can find meaning through engaging in pursuits that push you to your limit. Let's be honest: when you overcome an unsurmountable force, you look back on the experience and thank God it is over, but you are thankful for having overcome it because you grew as a person. I know you found joy in the experience because you exercised your will over you own nature and overcame an obstacle that seemed impossible. More specifically, you beat the odds and proved the doubters wrong. I love the quote by Bruce Lee where he states:

> *"The doubters said,*
> *"Man cannot fly,"*
> *The doers said,*
> *"Maybe, but we'll try,"*
> *And finally soared*
> *In the morning glow*
> *While non-believers*
> *Watched from below."*
>
> **— BRUCE LEE**

My question is this: What did you actually overcome? What did you really overcome? Because the warrior views an obstacle as insignificant. The issue is not the obstacle in front of you, because more times than not, it is the obstruction within your mind that holds you back. If life is perspective, then I have to know what your perspective is. Because perspective influences how you will perform. My perspective is that the obstacle that you will need to overcome is always you. You must learn to overcome yourself in order to achieve your personal life vision. What that means is you must begin to develop a daily personal assessment of yourself to understand what it is inside of you that is standing in the way of who you are supposed to become.

Have you sat down and done a gap analysis of your life? A gap analysis is when you identify your current situation and your future state. The future state represents who you want to become. Now anything in the middle is what you need to address to get to the better version of yourself.

Current State	Gaps	Future State
Who are you right now as of today?	What is holding me back from getting to my future state?	Who do you want to become in the future?

Your ultimate goal should be to work towards becoming the better version of yourself, and that is based on working towards being better every day. One of the first things I had to do was identify who I was and determine who I wanted to become. I made myself the project, I made my environment my personal laboratory, and I began assessing myself. Through the act of self-reflection, I began to recognize things about myself that would have been unobvious before. See, somewhere along the line, I lost myself. I lost my way, and as a result I lost my "why." But the real epiphany was my realization that I could craft a whole new me if I truly accepted and understood the guy I was and worked really, really, really hard to shape myself into the guy I wanted to become. My biggest issue in my life was I had lost sight and lost track of who I was and did not set the goals required to catapult me toward the future.

See, you and I are wired to be goal-directed; we are meaning-seeking individuals, driven to fulfill a purpose. We are made to perform at our highest potential and we need to continually learn and grow. That means that finding purpose is essential to existing, finding meaning is as essential as breathing; goals are just as important to life as eating. What that means is they are symbiotic, i.e. they all work together in shaping you into the person you "must become" to be truly fulfilled. So, have you identified goals that will move you closer to your desired end? Do you acknowledge that you can create the life you want?

CHAPTER 5

WHY MEANING IS IMPORTANT TO YOU

"Each man must look to himself to teach him the meaning of life. It is not something discovered: it is something molded."
—ANTOINE DE SAINT-EXUPERY

Here is why meaning is important. Meaning is a higher human need; it's a spiritually driven cognition, and it requires a higher state of awareness. It functions on a higher plane of consciousness and cannot be tapped into when your focus is on being basic. In fact, meaning relates to being significant and can be found through the act of work that is meaningful. Working with a purpose validates that you are here, and it helps you to find life's significance. Even if you are confused about "why" you are here, the desire to make your life mean something has everything to do with you seeking a significance for your life, because just like I wondered as a boy what my purpose was, you are likely wondering what is the purpose for your life too.

Honestly, the desire to know and understand was engineered into you before time began. You are designed to act, engage, and perform, and bear fruit. You were designed to create, explore, and subdue. You were made to be indomitable, you were made to be of service, and to put your whole-self into the act of engaging in a work or activity. So, what is my point? The point is this: the purpose of your life is to optimize every minute, every second, and every day doing things that are meaningful to you but also add value to the lives of others. You were designed to breathe life into others and not take away from them by being negative. The purpose is to serve something greater than yourself and to do all things for the glory of God. Maslow calls it self-transcendence, which comes from serving something or someone higher than you. Have you ever noticed that individual performance is elevated when it is directed toward someone or something that we find deeply meaningful to us? It is elevated when we find a cause for which we are willing to commit everything to. It is elevated when that cause becomes our reason for living.

In reality, a cause is really another way of describing a commitment to someone or something. So, let me ask you something: have you realized that you must find your true self and share your true self by serving somebody else? Because that is the way to get beyond yourself. Otherwise you will stay stuck in your own way. That means you have to be committed to improvement and serving. That is why you need to ask yourself: what are you really committed to? What is your motivation? I remember a commercial some years ago where a guy asked that very question in a humorous way. The problem was he wanted someone to give him motivation, but I am here to tell you that it is you who must find the motivation to live for something; it is you who must develop the resolve to be committed to something. Remember, it is your life and your commitment to yourself and that is the difference between winning and losing.

Commitment is important to engagement and meaning because it represents the emotional connection required to keep you linked to something or someone. A real purpose is identifiable by the depth of emotion that it produces within you. This is a surefire way of identifying if you are up to the challenge that is customarily required to achieve whatever you might choose to do. We can call that emotion a "passion," which is defined as "a strong feeling of enthusiasm or excitement for something or about doing something." When you have a passion for something or someone, you will do it, no matter the cost to you.

Secondly, when you feel a passion for something or someone, it reinforces within you just how badly you want it to happen; sometimes it is so strong, it feels as if you cannot have it you will cease to exist. The motivational speaker Eric Thomas sums it up this way: "You gotta succeed more than you want to breathe." So, you must ask yourself: how badly do I want this? What am I willing to do? What am I willing to give up to achieve this end? Sometimes it may seem as if you are mad or crazy, but the Wright Brothers were believed to be crazy for wanting to attempt to fly; they did it anyway. Accept that your idea or dream may not be popular. But the truth is the thought of not achieving your desired end should be more maddening than not even making the attempt. In his book *The Pursuit of Excellence*, Ted Engstrom tells the story of Winston Churchill. He talks about how Winston was an average student growing up, but Winston Churchill became one of the chief speakers in history. His advice to a group of young men was this: "Young men, never give up. Never give up! Never give up! Never, Never, Never, Never!"

You must never give up. It is a lot easier to keep focused attention when you are impassioned about a thing than to do it when you are not. See, a purpose or cause can be so strong that one is either able to overcome or sacrifice themselves in the act of trying to fulfill that cause, which leads to altruistic behaviors. For instance, soldiers perform selfless actions by risking lives for comrades and country while also killing the enemy. Actions of Japanese kamikaze pilots in World War II are examples of military sacrifice. So here is my question for you: have you found a cause for which you are willing to die? If you have, then you have found your reason for living and whatever that special thing is will give meaning to your life; and that life domain is where you want to place your mental energies. Because that is the place where you will find meaning and it will assist you in constructing a more meaningful life, and more importantly that is where you will excel and perform at an optimal level.

Now, what is that one thing that you are so passionate about that it keeps you awake at night? What is that one thing that you eat, sleep, and breathe? What is that one thing that makes you feel alive? Whatever that is, that is what will give you meaning in your life.

How to identify a passion

Identify what you would do if money was not an issue.

If you had a million dollars, what would you do? How would you spend your time?

What activities that you already do now for "free" would you continue to pursue and spend hours on even if no one paid you for doing them?

How can you use your passion to make the world a better place?

SO, WHAT IS MEANING, ANYWAY?

We are constantly seeking meaning. The beauty of seeking it is that it is obtained when you really begin to question your life and seek to find the meaning of it. Here is the truth about meaning: you will never be able to discover the meaning of life. The meaning of life is illusive and uniquely subjective. But you can identify what makes your life meaningful and do things that give your life a sense of meaning.

Mihaly Csikszentmihalyi, the author of *Flow*, suggests that life becomes a meaningful experience when our lives are directed toward a goal; but here is the key: a goal must be worthy of its pursuit for us to strive for it and for it to create meaning. That means that meaning is found in engaging in activities that stretch us mentally, physically, and spiritually. He also suggests that to experience a state of flow, one must be fully engaged in an activity where you are so lost in the moment that your whole being is working in perfect cadence, and you are experiencing complete enjoyment. It is a state of bliss. As a runner, I experience these moments. When these moments occur, I experience a mind, body, and spirit connection that is joyful. I forget myself. I just run on autopilot. It is in these moments I stop time. I don't reflect, I don't question, I simply flow. These are the moments when I feel whole, complete, and connected.

Now I know this form of engagement is directed toward physical pursuits, but it is important to understand that the real value of flow is the fact that you can create balance or harmony in your life when all your efforts are directed at optimizing your life experiences and toward a particular life goal. This is really what performance is all about, and it is a requirement for you to achieve the vision for your life.

Maybe the problem you are experiencing in your work or life is a loss of meaning because you have not set goals that challenge you, or you work in a job that simply does not provide you with growth. The greatest destroyer to human growth and increased performance is boredom caused by not being challenged. Maybe the problem is that you are not directing your potential toward crafting a vision for your life, so you have nothing to shoot for; you have nothing to live for. Maybe you should take my lesson on stars and think about how when I began to look up at the stars in that sky that night, I started to stretch my mind toward possibility. I felt a sense of joy as I stretched myself. I believe that every time you look upon nature, you see greatness, and it is merely a reflection of the beauty that is inside of you. How long will you wait to bring the potential out of you? How long will you deny that you are a beautiful, creative individual who possesses a gift for the world? And believe me, the world needs whatever you have. You know how I know? Because we are all given gifts to uplift others. But many of us squander our gifts and talents because we assume that they are not creative enough; we ignore them because we judge their value before we have even developed them to a point of maturity. Don't listen to the naysayers; they eventually become advocates of your cause. Just focus on developing your gift.

Sometimes we view them as too unusual, but maybe the gift is not the problem; the problem is that you are limiting yourself by not thinking about how you can creatively use them in work or life.

If creativity creates meaning, then that means that you are born with the capacity to create a meaningful life. It means you are more than capable of achieving ultimate mastery, and that is the eventual arrival at self-mastery and skill-mastery. It means you have the potential to create something beautiful, but it is not an object or a destination; it's simply the potential to become a better version of you and create a better life, but it requires changing your mental disposition.

THE REALITY OF MY LESSON ON STARS

Here is the reality of the lesson on stars: my father was simply watering the seed that was already buried inside of me. He did not know it. But that experience was meaningful because it made me question my life. Like me, your potential represents a slow-burning star, but it will eventually burn out if it is not cultivated through meaningful experiences. It is your responsibility to identify your personal significance, and that can only come from seeking to find your unique purpose or motivation for your life. Seeking purpose is a spiritual endeavor that requires learning to engage with the spiritual aspect of yourself. What that means is it is intrinsic and cannot be found in the pursuit of things. But it can be found through peak experiences.

WHAT ARE PEAK EXPERIENCES?

Abraham Maslow coined this term to describe nonreligious mystical experiences. Peak experiences are sudden feelings of intense happiness and well-being. Research shows that peak experiences tend to occur during artistic, athletic, or religious experiences. Moments in nature or during intimate moments with family or friends are also common. Achieving an important goal, either a personal or collective one, could also lead to a peak experience. Other moments when such experiences might occur include when an individual helps another person in need or after overcoming some type of adversity. The problem with our society is that many of us seek significance in the things we buy and not what is inside of us. Are you taking responsibility for the life you have? Are you exercising your will to meaning? Remember: meaning is found in experiencing something beautiful and that something beautiful is really just your ability to experience and seek to understand the significance of your life, and oftentimes what you seek does not cost anything. True happiness cannot be bought or bartered, because it has already been given to you freely. When you work on yourself, you have begun the process of building a beautiful life. The key is to begin the process of going beyond wanting to be basic and find a beautiful struggle; that struggle is you.

When you live your life with the goal of being the best version of yourself, you begin to live life fully engaged. You begin to achieve higher levels of work/life performance and this allows you to go beyond being ordinary and average to being exceptional or great.

In my opinion, exceptional performance comes from choosing your life path based on the difference it can make in the life of others. For the Native Americans, when they would come of age, they were encouraged to reflect on their purpose through a vision quest. In that time of reflection, the purpose was for them to seek a vision for their lives, and whatever was chosen was meant to be of benefit to themselves and to be a benefit to the world. This coming-of-age process was a rite of passage customary for signifying a transfer from adolescence to adulthood. But what is so valuable about the process of seeking a vision was that they learned to tie their work and life to the spiritual aspect of their natures. What they learned was that they possessed unique gifts and talents, and what they possessed was not to be used just for them; it was to be offered and given to meet the needs of their tribes. Similarly, this assisted them in living life with a focus on optimizing experiences and allowed them to go beyond being basic and average, because they learned to engage their whole selves in life.

What are your gifts? What do you love to do?	How can you use them to make the world better?

WHAT DOES IT TAKE TO BE ENGAGED IN OPTIMAL LIFE PURSUITS FOR ELITE LIFE PERFORMANCE?

Engagement is a big topic in the modern-day workforce, mostly because of the research of Gallup. They have studied the U.S., and even the global work environment, and found that the majority of people do not find their work to be meaningful or purposeful to their lives; the resulting work performance is thus diminished causing disengagement rather than engagement. Engagement is really just another word for performance.

No matter what you do, no matter the life domain, human performance is a requirement to live an optimal life. But the reality about the topic of engagement is that disengagement has existed for longer than you may think. Before it was called disengagement, it was called alienation, a feeling or sense that you are powerless. It is a feeling that you have no control over the decisions in your life. See, when you experience self-alienation, you have really lost a sense of self. You don't know who you are anymore. You lack the ability to identify what things are vital for you to thrive, grow, and develop. When this occurs, you lack the ability to make rational decisions to optimize your life. What I want you to become is a life athlete.

WHAT DOES IT MEAN TO BECOME A LIFE ATHLETE?

Here is the interesting thing about life: it refers to the concept of vitality. In fact, life means to possess spirit, passion, vigor, drive, and/or energy. The warrior seeks to engage and to be engaged in life, utilizing the whole person. The act of being fully engaged in life encompasses the mind, body, spirit and emotions in the act of living life and optimizing life. The act of engaging is done through engaging in pursuits that allow optimal life experiences. This is called being fully engaged in life, with the understanding that to be engaged in life is to live with the expectation that he or she participates in life whole-souled, with the mindset to overcome difficult obstacles in order to achieve an elite level of work/life performance. The popular definition of engagement is defined by the psychologist Vicktor Khan, who coined the name "engagement" in 1990 as "the harnessing of organization members' selves to their work roles; in engagement, people employ and express themselves physically, cognitively, and emotionally during role performances". What Khan is saying is that being fully engaged in work or life requires enlisting the whole self in the act of performing a particular task or role at an optimal level with the whole person involved in the process. This means we must develop all aspects of ourselves mind, body, spirt, and emotions if we are to experience heightened levels of work/life performance. Performing at the height of your abilities for you as the warrior requires (1) identifying your purpose or life goal, (2) identifying your talents or potentials, (3) learning how to actualize them, (4) and finally doing so with the objective of bringing them out of yourself, so that you are able to perform as an elite life athlete or a person with mastery over self and over one's craft. In reality, the two ideas go hand in hand. When you develop self-mastery, you are more effectively able to dominate a given activity and improve your quality of life. I love the wise words of King Solomon:

> *"A man's gifts make room for him and*
> *bring him before great men."*

If you study the top performers, what you will find is that they devote large amounts of their time to developing self-discipline, in order to develop mastery over their gifts or talents. They live, behave, and work with purpose and operate their lives based around their gifts. What they have done is fashion their professions around their innate abilities. The great warrior Miyamoto Musashi stated this about innate ability: "There is nothing outside of yourself that can ever enable you to get better, richer, stronger, or smarter. Everything is within. Everything exists. Seek nothing outside of yourself."

See, the warrior focuses on developing him/herself from the inside out, and this is uniquely different from learning to be proficient at a task. Develop internal mastery because elite performance comes from having an innate desire for achievement. So here is the difference between internal mastery and being externally driven to fulfill a goal:

Internal Mastery	External Goal Fulfillment
▪ See failure as a teaching tool	▪ Cannot accept failure
▪ View learning and development as life-long pursuit	▪ Do not learn from mistakes
▪ You are okay with performance, even if it is inching toward excellence	▪ Interprets failure as a sign of low ability and therefore predictive of future failure
▪ You seek out challenging new ways of developing your craft	▪ You require others to validate you and your performance
▪ You do not need an accolade, you are self-contained	

What is interesting about the potential for developing ultimate mastery is that when it comes from inside of you, it requires discipline, but it does not create stagnation. When it comes from inside of you, you become self-fueled because it is driven by the boundless energy that comes from spiritual resilience. This is the fire that causes you to always burn hot. This is what makes a warrior indomitable. I liken the desire for internal mastery to that of The Eternal Fires that are found in nature.

I recently read an article on eternal fires that have burned hot for centuries. Researchers do not know when they started burning but they estimate that some have been burning for over 6,000 years. I believe that when you begin to know yourself and know your purpose, you become self-fueled. You are always burning hot because you become fueled by your desire to achieve, to overcome, and to renew. See, a fire does not start out big; it is merely an ember, but given time, heat, and pressure, it becomes an unrelenting flame that feeds off itself. That is why it's important that you kindle the internal desire for mastery versus living for external goals. Internal mastery is the basis of longevity and staying power.

If what you are doing or how you are living or those that you are around take energy from you, if what you do does not give life to you, and if how you live does not focus on discipline, you are likely driven by external goal striving and eventually that flame will die. Someone who is externally driven is identifiable by how they approach mistakes. See, a warrior or elite life athlete operates from the spirit and what they are seeking to discipline is their spiritual nature through mental and physical means. Honestly, that is really what an athlete is meant to do. Their training and life experiences are all meant to transform them into a better version of themselves. To be great requires becoming disciplined.

DO YOU KNOW WHERE 'ATHLETE' COMES FROM?

Interestingly, athlete comes from the term 'asceticism.' Asceticism was initially a form of self-discipline that was customary for a nun or priest, someone who sought spiritual goals or to reach a higher spiritual plane. Ascetics generally required a severe level of self-discipline and avoidance of all forms of indulgence, typically for religious reasons. This term also comes from the Greek word askesis, which is translated as "exercise" or "training." It was primarily used by the Ancient Greeks to refer to the training that athletes underwent in preparation for competitions. The point of my mentioning this is that success is born from self-denial and self-sacrifice. If you want to overcome yourself, you must learn to strengthen the will. But far too few of us are willing to forgo short-term pleasure for long-term gains. So, we deny the calling we were designed for because it might mean struggling for a period of time in order to utilize how we are best gifted in work and life. The warriors of old understood the importance of discipline. Here is a truth about being disciplined: it leads to self-mastery, and self-mastery gives one the strength to achieve work mastery and arrive at a place of personal greatness.

These concepts are nothing new. They are timeless. In Roy Baumeister's book, *Willpower*, he discusses how David Blaine was inspired by men and women of the Victorian era. The Victorian era emphasized the importance of willpower and the ability to overcome the limiting barriers of one's instincts and impulses. But even before the Victorian Era and before David Blaine, self-mastery was a means to improve personal power for the Desert Fathers. And if you read about the life of Gandhi, you will find he spent much of his life performing rigorous experiments with the sole purpose of curbing his basic instincts so that he could operate on a higher plane. There must be something to adopting spiritual practices and walking a stricter path, because he became a major reason why India gained its independence. Yes, he may have started his salt march alone, but by the end the world was paying attention. Self-discipline has shown time and time again that we can override our emotions and instincts in order to realize higher levels of performance when we set our minds to will building.

THE WILL OF THE WARRIOR

For the warrior, the "will" is the single most important component to attaining self-mastery. Frankl identifies the will as a both a driver of one's life and a striving in one's life. Because the warrior is driven toward the desire to find meaning in life, and through the act of searching for meaning they develop mastery over themselves to obtain a particular goal or purpose. Warriors find meaning when they have successfully identified a purpose to strive for and begin directing all their energies toward the fulfillment of that end. The reality is that while the warrior seeks to obtain mastery, the true search is more concerned with experiencing meaning and identifying meaning in life. What I am saying is that through the act of expressing one's will, a warrior identifies his or her significance in life and is able to optimize his or her life potentials through the act of organizing their life around a unified "flow experience" to obtain a state of harmony in all areas of life. Warriors seek to engage their whole selves– mind, body, and spirit– in the pursuit of a purposeful goal to create ultimate meaning in life. Mihaly defines flow as "when an important goal is pursued with resolution, and all one's varied activities fit together into a unified flow experience; the result is that harmony is brought to consciousness".

While the warrior may engage in a life full of action, it is centered around the pursuit of life-mastery in order to create a complete flow experience, which is why warriors seek to identify purpose, and develop self-understanding and self-mastery over themselves, because only then can they arrive at a state of harmony or balance in their lives. Through developing a state of harmony, the warrior can acquire meaning in life and ultimate mastery. So, the warrior must develop (1) an ordered mind (2) intentionality and (3) the unity of feelings, actions, and thoughts to work in one accord to achieve a state of inner unity. Basically, what that means is that you only focus on what you can control. What you can control is inside of you.

Because the warrior seeks to create a state of flow in life, the continual exercising of mastery over one's self is essential. In order to create a harmonious life, it is important to identify will for what it is. The will is identifiable in three ways: the will to pleasure, the will to power, and the will to meaning.

The will to pleasure – Do you appeal to freedom to experience pleasure and avoid pain? While pleasure is a driver of human experience, when we let it consume us, it becomes our master. In coaching sessions, I listen as my clients lament the goals that they have that go unfulfilled because they are too involved in the pursuit of pleasurable experiences. The desire for pleasure overrides their want to grow into the better version of themselves. Pleasure becomes the power over them. It becomes the driving force for their lives. It becomes the reason why they exist.

The will to power – Do you exercise your right to power over yourself or others? Many of us seek to wield power or control over others in order to make ourselves feel important. This desire for control comes in the form of keeping someone else from their goals, imposing views and beliefs on others, and disregarding another person in order to get what you want. This form of power is a perversion of power. The true will to power is the power to exercise authority over one's own person. It should not focus on exercising authority over another for selfish reasons. A desire for power should revolve around developing one's self-mastery and skill mastery in order to achieve ultimate mastery.

THE WILL TO MEANING

While the will can be expressed through acting on desire for pleasure and it can be exercised through the act of power wielding, the true objective of the will to power is to be directed toward "finding and fulfilling one's meaning and purpose" in life. In effect, the warrior is driven to pursue a path of meaning and personal significance, in order to actualize performance and balance the tension between pleasure and power by focusing on empowering or exercising will over oneself, skill development, and serving others.

Sadly, too many of us focus on either pleasurable experiences or power-wielding over others instead of pursuing meaning and personal improvement. You will never develop Arête or excellence if you spend your time controlling others, allowing your irrational thoughts to control you, or seeking life purpose through the pursuit of pleasure, because they do not create personal significance. In the end, they only keep you from greatness. Stop limiting your performance! Will-building is a process of training ourselves mentally, physically, and spiritually to overcome obstacles and preform at optimal levels even in the face of overwhelming stress or under great pressure. If you want to overcome, you must train your whole person to be prepared to respond to unpredictable situations.

WHAT DOES THAT MEAN?

Well, it means that you must train your whole person to be adaptable to changing environments; you must place yourself in uncomfortable situations and find ways to switch up things. Because what decreases performance is too much predictability. You must learn to disrupt your own thinking.

One thing that is important to realize about David Blaine is that he possesses a passion for his craft and works to master himself. So, maybe hard work may not make you an elite performer in a sport, but it certainly will assist you in being a better leader, entrepreneur, or elite life performer.

While this may seem obvious, the reality is that so few of us are living, working, and experiencing life fully engaged, and this is primarily because most of us do not find meaning or satisfaction in our lives. We are not aligning our work and lives around our talents because we have not asked the question: What is my purpose in life? We simply have no idea what we are here to do, nor do we know what we are capable of, so how can you craft a vision when your life is largely unexamined? What happens is you experience the existential void and you become stuck, depressed, and stagnant.

EXISTENTIAL VOID

The late Viktor Frankl suggested that humanity is experiencing an existential crisis. An existential crisis is when one experiences a deep unsettling feeling at the core of one's self. It is a state of questioning, where you are forced to ask, "who am I," why am I here," "what is my purpose" and "am I living my purpose?" Unfortunately, the majority of our world is experiencing this, in the form of a spiritual crisis. The problem is most of us ignore the question of existence. We are on a road with no clear destination. We just know we are walking with little to no understanding of what we are walking to or what we want to actually achieve in life. We have set no goals, so life just happens to us.

TO NOT SEEK TO UNDERSTAND CREATES A VOID

In my coaching sessions, without fail, these questions always come up. So many people lack an understanding of purpose and where they are going. The truth is, every one of us is concerned about where we are going. We all want to know that what we are doing is purposeful and adds value to our own lives and the lives of others. But what is interesting is that many of us live our lives unaware that we are in this existential vacuum or are experiencing a void within us. This existential vacuum can be summed up as a hole that we seek to fill with anything and everything we think will make us feel full. We seek completeness but not within ourselves. While we may fill this emptiness with something, it never provides us with the ultimate sense of meaning or purpose we seek, because what you seek can't be found through external means. The end result is a feeling of meaninglessness.

This feeling of meaningless is nothing new; it was identified as alienation by the Communist thinker Karl Marx; today we call it disengagement, but what it amounts to is that somewhere along the line you lost sight of who you were and stopped dreaming about who you could become. So you experience a deep rift between who you are and who you are meant to become. You must begin the process of reacquainting yourself with yourself and seek a life of substance.

WHAT IS MEANINGLESSNESS?

A life void of substance is a meaningless life. This void has to do with a need to better direct our future and ultimately do something meaningful with our lives. The problem with most individuals is that they seek to fill the void in their lives with stuff. The warrior does not seek stuff; he or she seeks substance. How do you give life substance? Well, you do this by focusing on making meaningful experiences in work and life.

The reality is that what we seek is spiritual and not physical. We seek to live for a higher purpose or higher ideals. The reality is that things of substance are usually intrinsic in nature. They are not bought with money. What gives us the most meaning in our lives is the pursuit of worthwhile experiences that promote personal growth and development. We find fulfillment in higher pursuits or higher ideals. It is through living with these higher ideals that the journey of one's life becomes worth experiencing and examining. So let me ask you a few questions: do you understand what it means to be a warrior? Do you know what warriorship is or how to begin the process of finding purpose? Well, it is time to begin to answer the existential questions, because these questions are the basis for enhancing human performance and tapping into the essence of your talents. It is with these questions that you will begin the journey of warriorship, or the road to renovatio.

When I look back now, the questions I asked myself were also the questions I asked Bill, one of my very first coachees. What is interesting about exploring these questions is that in every conversation I have had with a business owner, a leader, or just the average person, not one person I encountered could answer the question of purpose before starting coaching. What is apparent is that these questions are the basis for improving work/life performance because they are the basis for existence. When these questions go unanswered, you become like a ship at sea with no captaining at the helm, and that just won't do.

THE SHIP WITHOUT A RUDDER

You may feel as Bill felt at the beginning of his road to renovatio or self-renewal. He was frustrated with the direction of his life and described himself like a boat out to sea without a rudder, on a course but with no idea where he was going or when he would arrive; all he knew was he was in a boat that he admitted he was not steering. The boat was being blown by the wind and he was floating along. But even worse, he was stuck lacking direction. He was unhappy, he felt powerless, and did not know what he was capable of. He was stuck.

You don't typically perform your best at what you do not enjoy, and you cannot set goals when you don't know what you seek to achieve. But maybe the problem is you are not pursuing your calling or simply not seeking the purpose of your life because you have never sat down and explored what your talents are. You have not asked the essential question which is: why am I here? Simply put, if you do not know yourself, how can you grow yourself? You can't know your purpose if you do not know your person. Thus, you can never truly optimize your life potentials.

Answer These Existential Questions

- Who am I?

- Why am I here?

- What is my purpose in life?

- Am I living my purpose?

- Am I optimizing my gifts and talents?

- What do I want my life to be? What are my goals?

- What can I do to improve my work performance and life performance?

CHAPTER 6

DO YOU KNOW YOUR POTENTIAL?

"The will to win, the desire to succeed, the urge to reach your full potential... these are the keys that will unlock the door to personal excellence."
—CONFUCIUS

If you want to know your potential, I suggest you begin to journal your experiences and how you react to things. This will help you identify your likes, dislikes, and areas of giftedness. One of my favorite management gurus, Peter Drucker, wrote a book titled *Managing Oneself*. In the book, Drucker discusses the importance of assessing one's self through what he calls "feedback analysis". Really, feedback analysis is the recording of your day-to-day experiences in a personal renovatio journal. I have done this for over eleven years. In fact, I encourage you to do it if you want to be able to analyze your life events, record progress on goals, and review what goals you have achieved year after year. Also, it is important to review what obstacles you overcame on the way to achieving a goal for your life. But first it is good to set SMART goals. Goal setting multiplies the likelihood of goal achievement. According to Dr. Gail Matthews, a psychology professor at Dominican University in California, who did a study on goal-setting with 267 participants. Individuals were randomly assigned to various groups. The study compared the difference in achievement between those who wrote down their goals compared to those that didn't. She found that the participants who spent time writing down their goals experienced a 42% increase in goal achievement. Dr. Matthews also found that when accountability was incorporated into the process of writing down goals the rate of successful goal achievement rose to a 78%. A major key to achieving greatness is setting goals. If you are not where you want to be it might be time to set SMART goals. Take a minute to set your SMART goals.

Verify that your goal is SMART

Specific: What exactly will you accomplish?

Measurable: How will you know when you have reached this goal?

Achievable: Is achieving this goal realistic with effort and commitment? Do you have the resources to achieve this goal? If not, how will you get them?

Relevant: Why is this goal significant to your life?

Timely: When will you achieve this goal, identify a date, time, etc.

MY FEEDBACK ANALYSIS RITUAL

I have a yearly ritual of reviewing all my journals, starting with my very first journal to my most recent one. The journals are my story and a record of how I dealt with life trials and an assessment of lessons learned, and the blessings that I experienced throughout the years. I would suggest that you begin journaling your life experiences. Do you keep a journal? Go get one and start the process. You will thank me for it because you will develop a better understanding of yourself.

Drucker suggested that to operate at a higher level of performance, you must learn your strengths and your weaknesses. That is what the journal will teach you to identify. I began journaling because I wanted to record my life. I realized that I had been doing very little to understand who I was at my core. I now realize that journaling helped me to identify my character flaws and work toward overcoming them. We are enslaved by our character flaws, but journaling is a means to bring these flaws to light.

Journaling is a freeing experience. It will allow you to lay down the weights you have been carrying around. The most beautiful aspect of journaling is seeing where you have come from. See, life is nothing more than situations thrown at you. You are given various options, but no matter the option, you will always be responsible for the wins and losses you incur. I journal because it helps me to see how I am progressing as a life athlete on my warrior path. This is a form of daily renewal or renovatio that I do without fail because like you, I desire to be more, do more, and achieve more. But more importantly, journaling helps you to see how you have overcome the irrational beliefs you carry in your head, because what every man and woman fights is themselves. I can remember the first time in my life I determined that I wanted to overcome myself. What I had to overcome was my mindset:

Change your mindest by journaling

For professional athletes, it is a means of assessing their deliberate practice in the field of sports performance. Pro athletes like Serena Williams and Michael Phelps journal in order to reflect on their practice, according to Richard Kent based on his article entitled, "Learning from Athletes' Writing: Creating Activity Journal." In the article Richard Kent stated this:

"Tennis great Serena Williams keeps a journal. At Wimbledon 2007, she shared a few pages of her writing with reporters. "Writing," she explained, "can help clear out negative thoughts and emotions that keep you feeling stuck" (Williams and Williams 114). Olympic swimming phenom Michael Phelps spoke about his reflective journal with The Today Show host Matt Lauer just after the 2012 summer games (Stump). The all-time Olympic medal winner kept the journal to preserve his memories."

The foremost authority on journaling, Dr. James Pennebaker, suggested that "when people write about major upheavals they begin to organize and understand them," which eventually allows them to "move beyond the trauma." He further suggested that, "if you can get people to talk or write about their problems, their health improves."

Journaling is a practice that you can use to improve your mind and even alter your mental state and you can track your life progression year over year. You will see how much your mindset has changed because you will have a record of your progress.

A FIXED MIND

> *"Victorious warriors win first and then go to battle, but defeated warriors go to war first and then try to figure out how to win."*
>
> **- MIYAMOTO MUSASHI**

Mindsets are beliefs or views you have about yourself. The beliefs can either be true or false. The key is learning to recognize the beliefs that are true and learning to let go of the beliefs that are false. We call such beliefs irrational beliefs. They impact your performance because, according to the famed psychologist Albert Ellis. An irrational belief does the following:

1. It misrepresents truth.
2. It is unreasoned.
3. It prevents you from reaching your goals.
4. It leads to unwholesome feelings.
5. It leads to self-sabotaging behavior.

At the heart of our irrational beliefs is an inability to accept who we are and who we are not. I think back, and I realize that I suffered from irrational beliefs that distorted my understanding of who I was, and distorted beliefs about yourself will take you off your path. Sadly, any of us who are not walking our own unique paths we are taking the path of least resistance instead of taking the narrow path of purpose.

Now, every one of us is born with the desire to take our own path, but few are equipped to take up the task of identifying what that path is that they must take. The culprit of purpose is fear, fear of discomfort, fear of failure, fear of rejection, fear of being hungry, fear of losing family, fear of not finding what one was seeking to obtain, fearful thinking. Quite honestly, too many of us are ruled by fear because we simply lack the faith and strength of will to achieve our desired purpose. We are just too afraid of doing what it requires, which is delving into the depths of ourselves to confront the sunken ships of disappointment.

Recently I was reading a book by Eileen Flanagan titled *The Wisdom to Know the Difference* and she made a profound statement that relates to this concept of delving into the depths of ourselves. Eileen is an Irish-American and is very in touch with Irish Folklore and she stated that it was customary for old Irish fishermen to lack the necessary skill to swim because they believed that it did not matter; they were powerless to the God of the sea and if and when he took a fisherman, they believed in their heart of hearts that there was nothing they could do. What is so impactful about this analogy is that it represents the duality of being human; like these fishermen, we lessen our will when we do not confront our pasts, we give away our power when we do not develop the needed skills to reclaim our personal power. When we fail to change our situations knowingly, it is evident that there are mental strongholds that keep us from developing the abilities required to overcome the polarities of our lives.

Strongholds are barriers. They are built in our minds to keep negative beliefs in and positive beliefs out. These strongholds can only be broken when they are challenged. As you can see from the example of these fishermen, a false belief about ourselves can be so strong that it binds us and tricks us into believing that we cannot do better; it holds us so tightly that it restricts our ability to think rationally and takes away our personal power. It leaves us in a perpetual struggle to champion the waters of life without a life jacket. That is not elite living and ensures you never champion success. Our beliefs create our reality. Our beliefs are so entrenched in our unconscious mind that we would rather die than let them go, because to let them go means having to change patterns of behavior. The power of choice is useless when you choose to stay powerless to your beliefs.

These fishermen had a choice to accept their fate or change the way they approached their work and it would have likely improved their ability to survive the waves of life's sea, but they found comfort in a state of powerlessness. Why wouldn't they want to relieve that tension? Why would they not have taken a different path? They accepted the idea they were powerless. The reality was this was an irrational belief that they accepted as truth.

If you can identify any such behaviors, then it is safe to say that your performance is being hampered by an irrational belief that you hold in your mind.

Beliefs are very powerful, and it is important you recognize what your beliefs are because they drive performance. A major reason my life was less than stellar was that I operated in a state of disbelief. I did not utilize the power of faith. Faith allows you to live in the now and work toward a future, but disbelief leaves you stuck in the past that can never achieve a future future goal state.

Great performers utilize visualization as a means to achieve their goals. Did you know that the great soccer player Pele would sit and visualize with vividness himself playing before every soccer match? Why can't you do the same? Physical or deliberate practice combined with visualization, positive self-talk, and creating vivid pictures of a particular performance are excellent ways to prepare your whole person to realize a dream.

In fact, when an athlete does mental training, the athlete is taught to be future-focused; they are taught to dial into the here and now but begin to visualize the future they want. They are taught how to shift their mental perspectives about themselves and visualize a future state. Are you visualizing your future by practicing through visualization?

Every day, take a moment and utilize mental imagery and visualization. If you can see it in your mind, then you can achieve it in your life.

"Guang Yue, an exercise psychologist from Cleveland Clinic Foundation in Ohio, compared people who went to the gym with people who carried out virtual workouts in their heads," she said. "The group of participants who conducted mental exercises of the weight training increased muscle strength by almost half as much (13.5 percent). This average remained for three months following the mental training." (Visualization is a powerful tool.)

In another study done by Pascual-Leone, A., Nguyet, D., Cohen, L. G., Brasil-Neto, J. P., Cammarota, A., & Hallett, M. (1995) It was found that participants who mentally practiced a 5-finger piano arrangement on an imagined piano for two hours a day had the same (neural changes and reduction of mistakes) as the participants who physically practiced the same passage on an actual piano.

Visualization is the technique used by the Navy SEALs, martial artists, and runners. In fact, this is one that I learned as a young runner, but for whatever reason, I didn't see the application of it to my personal life until I had to do my dissertation. Well, it must have worked.

Mental imagery is used successfully to assist victims of strokes to rehabilitate themselves. You can literally use your mind to succeed in actual life. There are four elements to mental imagery - Relaxation, Realism, Regularity and Reinforcement. We call these the 4Rs (relaxation, realism, regularity, reinforcement):

TRY THE 4RS

How To Visualize

Relaxation – relax your mind and body using diaphragmic breathing.

Realism – engage all your senses (sights, sounds, smells, tastes, touches) to make the experience as real as possible.

Regularity - Spend about 10 minutes a day practicing imagery. Repetition, concentration, and focus are key to the process.

Reinforcement – To reinforce or imprint the vision on your subconscious you must encode it into your mind. This can be done by placing the vision on a wall, writing it in a journal and reviewing it daily, and just verbally describing the scenario so that it becomes ingrained in your subconscious mind.

NOW I NEED YOU TO LISTEN FOR THE LESSON.

This in itself is a lesson. No matter the domain, the reality is that if you really analyze techniques or skills that you have learned over your life, what you may find is that these skill sets are applicable to various areas of your life. The samurai Miyamoto Musashi would tell you that, while we are quick to build knowledge, the true impact of knowledge is when it becomes wisdom. In turn, wisdom allows us to know when to apply what we have learned in our lives. This requires a change in mindset.

If you are thinking right now that you need to make a change, you are right. Your mindset needs to change if you are to increase performance and realize the extent of your talents. What you are experiencing is a fixed mindset. According to Carol Dwek, author of *Mindset*, you can possess one of two different mindsets. You can either possess a fixed mindset or a growth mindset. Based on her research she found that:

> *"Students who believed their intelligence could be developed (a growth mindset) outperformed those who believed their intelligence was fixed (a fixed mindset). And when students learned through a structured program that they could 'grow their brains' and increase their intellectual abilities, they did better. Finally, we found that having children focus on the process that leads to learning (like hard work or trying new strategies) could foster a growth mindset and its benefits."*

Understand that human potential is infinite; it is never really stuck. See, when something possesses potential, it always has promise, but it requires a stimulant to get it to become active. If you have found yourself to be stuck, then you are likely at a point in your life that requires you to "make a decision" about the direction of your life. Upon making whatever decision you are grappling with, you will be required to "take that decision" and stick with it; and if you want to pull the potential out of you, you must set goals that are hard because struggle breeds success.

YOUR MIND MUST STAY ON PURPOSE

Here is the reality: what is stuck and needs constant renewal is the point of your personal renovatio. It's a renewal of your mind. You must recognize that it is your mind that is your enemy when you do not develop a process for renewing it. If you don't possess a growth mindset, you will never overcome your personal plateaus because every battle begins in the mind. It is acted out in one's behaviors; the proof of how you are doing in the war for your mind is in the everyday experiences and the quality of your life. When you fail to prepare your mind for each day, when you fail to improve yourself a little more each day, you are setting yourself up to lose before you even enter the ring of life. Go beyond acquiring knowledge. You must learn to cultivate wisdom. Wisdom arrives through trial and error.

That is why you must learn to stay ready, so that you never have to get ready, and this requires commitment to a cause. Honestly it takes courage to work on yourself and it takes great heart to dare to dream. That is why your purpose has to be bigger than you are.

Purpose gives you the energy to soldier on, even when everything and everyone around you is telling you to stop. When people tell you to stop, you are usually going in the right direction; but when you are told to stop, don't stop on your road. Reject the negativity but translate what they are actually saying: I want you to stop living because I have stopped living. I want you to stop dreaming because I have stopped dreaming, I want you to be broken because my spirit is broken. Malcom Forbes stated, "When you cease to dream, you cease to exist." If we are here to exist, then the question is: when are you going to start living out your dream? You have to cease to just dream, because if dreaming is all you are doing then you are really in a state of delusion. You must become aware of your personal significance and then pursue your purpose with extreme prejudice. You must be aggressive. You must!

ARE YOU AWARE OF YOUR SIGNIFICANCE?

You see, to know your worth is to understand you have value. Now maybe you are aware of your significance, but the key is to make it known to those around you; this requires recognizing what your gifts are and understanding that the warrior works from a trajectory no different than any other warrior throughout time. Every warrior lived and died for a cause. Like these great men and women before you. You travel a road no different than Gandhi, Martin Luther King, Jr., Mother Teresa, Joan of Arc and so many throughout history that have either traveled or are traveling on this road to spiritual growth, personal development, and immovableness. Those who have traveled it lived their years fully engaged in the work of their lives. Those who are still here are living lives centered around being and becoming all they are meant to be. The only difference between those who are great and those who are not is they found a cause to fight for and they found a reason to live. They found an area within life's domain where they could express their fullest potentials.

See, Frankl identified the crisis of our time as being "a man who simply exists without a true cause or purpose for his or her existence." It is not the fact that we lack ideals but that we have lost the will to fight for what we believe in. Because many of us do not have a cause to fight for, we do not possess a cause that will assist us in finding our meaning in work, nor can many of us identify what is required to pursue that which is meaningful in our lives. How can you find meaning when you do not know who you are authentically? How can one find meaningful work if one does not seek it out? The problem is that for far too long, you have viewed yourself as an average man or woman; but the reality is that you are more than average. You possess seeds of potential, but you must find your cause. See, when you find something to truly live for, that is what will give you internal strength to fight for it, and even die for it. It is time you identify the thing for which you will live. A real cause is not a company, it is not a place, it not a destination; honestly, the cause is you. The late famous poet Miguel Pinero stated in his poem about seeking a cause:

> *"he died seekin' the cause*
> *he died seekin' a Cause*
> *he died deaf dumb & blind*
> *he died & never found his Cause*
> *because you see he never knew*
> *that he was the Cause."*

It is time to ask yourself if you are the cause, because if you are the cause, then you are the answer. The question is: what is the cause you are seeking or purpose for which you would live or die? If you could find the thing for which you would lay down your life, then you have found your reason to live. I hope you recognize it is you who must seek; and through the act of seeking within yourself, you will find the purpose that was uniquely designed just for you. How can one change the world outside of them if they do not change the world within first? Because what comes out of you is what defines you. Jesus stated it best when He said, "First take the log out of your own eye, and then you will see clearly to take out the speck that is in your brother's eye."

Perhaps we must begin to look at ourselves first before we hope to develop the true potential in others. It is time to reflect on you. See, a great travesty of human existence is that we focus more on the accomplishments of others but give too little attention to the potential within our own selves. We read everyone's history but our own; we will read about the greatness of others but only scratch the service of realizing the greatness within us.

I have clients who can tell me in detail the life and history of a great football player, they can speak with passion about the newest technology, and identify the strengths and weaknesses of political candidates. They are able to tell me the person's history and recount their life story. They can identify what made a leader great but what they are not good at is telling their story. They simply lack the self-knowledge to know what makes them great. The reason for this is obvious: they have not taken the time to reflect on their lives. Why? It is far easier to live vicariously through someone else than to actively pursue yourself with the same vigor or passion, because it is hard work, it is scary, and when you dive into the depths of yourself, you uncover truth.

Now, I know the truth will set you free. But here is the truth about truth: truth is scary because it means you or I have to change something about ourselves. I think it is easier to live in comfortable enslavement at times than to actually experience the uncomfortableness of being free to change. Yes, truth is freedom, but for many of us it requires changing our lives and that is a fearful thing.

See, you were never meant to live life telling his-story or her-story. You were meant to uncover and report on *your* story. Warriors seek themselves because they recognize their true potential is in the power of being aware of who they are and who they are not. Finding your own path is the gift given to you. It is a choice to take a path of your choosing. I believe that ignoring truth conditions you to adapt to circumstances that kill your soul. Truth sets you free, and though it does cause discomfort for a time, the discomfort is temporary.

I was reading a book by my mentor and friend Ari Weinzweig, titled *Managing Ourselves*. Ari is the president of Zingerman's Community of Businesses in Ann Arbor, Michigan. He is one of the most interesting and unique men I have come across. I don't know too many CEOs who manage a 550-million-dollar company and pour water in the restaurant that they own. Trust me, it is not a gimmick. Ari possesses a strong sense of self and knows what it means to take a personal path, an authentic path based on one's personal vision for their life. In fact, he travels extensively, teaching on the topic of envisioning. Ari states, "When we follow a prescribed path by others... a future outside of our souls is never compelling". Rather he states that there is a freedom, a lightness of being, and a compelling energy that comes from doing things we believe in and going after life the way we want to live in a grounded, generous, and just way. The reality of your life is that it is yours and you have the power to change it. The warrior understands this all too well.

PART 2
SELF-UNDERSTANDING – TRUTH

CHAPTER 7

FEAR OF LIVING

There are no contests in the Art of Peace.
A true warrior is invincible because he or she
contests with nothing. Defeat means to defeat the
mind of contention that we harbor within.
— **MORIHEI UESHIBA**

What is most important for you as a warrior is to understand yourself. This is done through developing self-understanding. A simpler interpretation of the self is that it is your perceptions, emotions, personal experiences, thoughts, and feelings derived from both your conscious and unconscious mind. The self is who you are and defines how you live, what you believe, and drives your behaviors. The self is you. You are a system of interworking parts that make up a whole. A warrior understands that a whole system works effectively when it is unified. You are a system of one. The question is: are you in full alignment? Are you truly conscious? Are you aware that you are more than the sum of your parts? To be truly alive, you must be whole. It is time you identified your true self so that you can overcome fear.

Human beings commonly identify the true self based on specific behaviors which create one's self-concept. Self-concept is an intrinsic psychological depiction of the person which encompasses how one classifies himself in comparison to other human beings, other social networks, and the cultural norms that have shaped a particular individual's self-identity or one's authentic self. The concept of the true self or authentic self is linked to the human drive to find meaning or significance in one's life by the act of being authentic or true to one's personal belief, values, or spirit. Warriors are true to purpose and actively engage in the purpose of their lives. They do not fear living because they have accepted that one day they will die.

The authentic self is a mediator of one's actions: (1) it shapes how one views the existence of another person, (2) impacts perceptions about the meaning of one's life, (3) and affects the choices one makes. Having a positive view of one's self determines how one creates meaning in their lives and influences overall satisfaction in life. The Gallup poll found that highly engaged workers find their work meaningful and their lives purposeful when the work is viewed as important or meeting a higher purpose.

As a warrior, your life must be less about money and more about meaning. Your greatest fulfillment will always come from what you give and not what you receive. To overcome fear, you must begin to understand yourself. A warrior works day after day to overcome negativity. To overcome yourself, you must first understand yourself. Improving your self-understanding is essential to the process of taking the path of warriorship. A lack of self-understanding ensures that you will never answer your calling in life, because to understand a life direction requires understanding who you are and what your core beliefs and values are. If you lack self-understanding, you will lack the self-knowledge required to know what is necessary for you to find direction and make the decisions that are in line with who you are at your core. Self-understanding is the basis for the warrior's strength. It is through self-knowing that a warrior develops personal power to experience the outside world. See, self-understanding is the foundation for acquiring personal power.

If you do not know yourself, how can you identify your talents and gifts? But the flipside of understanding yourself is that you have to face your fears. Because it is when you face fear that you begin to understand what you are capable of. You must understand your perceived limits and get beyond them.

> *"If you always put limits on everything you do, physical or anything else, it will spread into your work and into your life. There are no limits. There are only plateaus, and you must not stay there. You must go beyond them."*
>
> **- BRUCE LEE**

To actualize the human potential, a warrior must develop his or her personal power. In Greek, the word for power is 'dunamis,' which means "force," an act of power to be dynamic, or to be dynamite. It is the warrior's personal human potential that is sought to be actualized. To become a warrior, your life must be focused around dunamis to become personally powerful, personally explosive, and personally dynamic; but this can only be actualized through developing purpose, self-understanding, self-mastery, and harmony, i.e. the PUSH that equates to developing an immovable mind, ready and prepared for any and all things. Another way of describing this is "to develop an immoveable mind that is unfettered." While being immovable means to be unwavering, willing and ready for any and all things, to be unfettered means to be free of restrictions; it means to let the mind flow freely without restrictions. You must become aware of what is holding you back in your life.

The greatest restriction on the average man or woman is possessing a mind of fear because fear restricts the forward progression of the warrior and disallows the warrior to act with intention and execute their goals with impeccability or complete "flow," which is a completely focused motivation. It is a single-minded immersion and represents perhaps the ultimate experience in harnessing emotions in the service of performing and learning. In flow, the emotions are not just contained and channeled, but positive, energized, and aligned with the task at hand. The hallmark of flow is a feeling of spontaneous joy, even rapture, while performing a task, although flow is also described as a deep focus on nothing but the activity – not even oneself or one's emotions. This is essential to developing impeccability.

"True Power is Derived From True Focus"

IMPECCABILITY

Historically the warrior is known for being impeccable or seeking to achieve the highest level of human performance. The Greeks called this Arête, which refers to excellence of any kind. The act of training and development was utilized to develop the mind, body, spirit, and emotional management of a man or woman, in order to mold them into impeccable warriors who were flawless in combat. However, in the modern-day context, our focus on warriorship refers to the successful navigation of one's overall meaning in life and the execution and attainment of goals and tasks. But to find meaning in life requires the warrior to be fully engaged in the process of being present in the act of living life. Obtaining ultimate meaning in life is the aim of the warrior and it is essential for the warrior to direct all efforts toward this aim. While there are many ways of finding meaning in life, and although it is different for everyone and every warrior, work is one way of finding meaning. Finding meaning in work is actually one way to find meaning in one's life. While it is not the only way, it is pretty important when you consider the fact that you will spend more time in your life working than you will any other place. Yep, work matters to life and that is why it is important to find your life's work and pursue it.

You cannot hope to become a warrior if you are being held back by fear, because a warrior must always PUSH forward. But to become a warrior, it begins with first knowing thyself. You cannot actualize your power potential until you come full circle with who you are and who you are not. When something is actualized, it means to become real. It means to take a thought, idea, or concept that resides within and give it life. The power I speak of is not the power to dominate another because that is tyranny; rather I speak of the ability to exhibit personal power or dominance over one's own self and take back your will.

Here is another reality: to become a champion requires overcoming your personal nature. Personal mastery is arrived at by exercising personal will over your mental state, because only then can you overcome your current circumstances; only then can you overcome your fears and physical desires.

Which leads to the questions of: How much power do you have over your person? How much of your power do you give away? Have

121

you developed the creative power to formulate an independent idea and bring it to life? As an entrepreneur, leader, and meaning-seeker, your ability to be an effective warrior requires learning to develop your will over yourself. You must learn to take back your mind through self-mastery so that you can achieve skill-mastery. You must learn to improve your attentional focus. Improving focus leads to increased will.

BUILD SELF-RELIANCE

You cannot find your significance in others, and seeking to be validated by others can derail greatness within you. You must develop self-reliance. Successful individuals are oftentimes misunderstood, and more times than not laughed at. They are bound by a continual striving to find meaning in life by staying focused on their personal vision even when it means forgoing pleasure and external power. What the warrior wants is to arrive at a state of harmony within and reflect this outwardly. When you become self-led, you will become self-made and you will be a servant to others. Warriors act with selfless motives. For me, I had to learn to live for something greater than myself and to act for that higher cause. I act and live with a focus on the spirit and I allow myself to be transformed daily and renewed daily by the spirit of truth. The only way to attain this form of discipline is to be self-reliant and to focus on learning better and more effective ways to lead your person.

SELF-LEADERSHIP AND TIME

A warrior possesses the ability to lead oneself. In the world of work and life, we call it self-leadership, but for centuries it has always been understood by the warrior class as the ability to master one's mind, body, and spirit. Self-led men and women recognize their minds are powerful. Harnessing the power of their minds is essential to developing the competencies required to will themselves and not be willed by their body and mind, because they focus more on spiritual development.

The authors of *Self-leadership*, Andrew Bryant and Ana Lucia Kazan, describe the concept of self-leadership as an exercise of deliberately prompting one's thoughts, emotions, and actions to realize an objective. Warriors and self-led individuals possess the internal drive; they are more able to exercise their freedom of choice, they are more adept at solving problems, and possess an immovable mind. This is what is meant by being a warrior. Warriors are self-led and do not seek to find their significance in others. They find that others possess significance, but the significance that they seek comes from knowing themselves and appreciating the strengths of others; but their focus is on developing their own talents and capabilities, because they believe that they too are endowed with God-given gifts that will allow them to overcome the challenges of their own lives. I believe that far too many of us focus on competing against others as a means to attain significance. But the reality is that the real means to achieve significance is seeking and finding the significance in ourselves over time and finding ways to create synergies with those with whom we keep company. Don't ever let someone take your personal power. This happens when you seek for them to validate you.

See, our greatest victories are when we have reclaimed what we have lost and more times than not, that is our own personal sense of self. To renew your mind is the beginning of finding your own personal power. This is what renovatio represents; it does not represent competing against another because the greatest opponent you will ever have is you. You must overcome yourself. Reclaim what you have lost and stop giving it away.

WHO ARE YOU REALLY COMPETING WITH?

I remember as a boy the first time I recognized the purpose of an opponent. As a track runner, you learn a lot about life through running. In fact, you learn the secret to success in work and life. Success is determined not by intelligence alone but by developing a mindset that is as fluid as the act of running, which is how running taught me to understand the concept of PUSH. Coach Kerner was in his 50s and could run with us in sprints. I remember him telling me that your focus is never on your opponent, because what you are racing against is time. Time doesn't wait for any man. It does not eat, it does not sleep, it never takes a break, and no matter how fast you run, you will never out work it. Therefore, time is the greatest competitor because it cannot be beaten. In fact, you could say it is the great equalizer because every headstone I have ever seen shows one's date of birth and their date of final rest. So, no matter how victorious you are in your race, remember that time will never wait for you.

Why then are you worrying about the man in the lane next to you when it is time that is always in front of you? I can hear him tell me, "Stay in your lane, Amos. Run your own race." Self-leadership and self-development are essential to attaining your goals and that is what warriors do. They seek to exercise mastery over their minds, bodies, and spirits and this is the way of life and it is called warriorship.

The interesting thing about mastery is when it is developed, it becomes noticeable to others. See, the way of the warrior within revolves around elevating yourself from an average to an elite level of performance in work and life. The warrior focuses on being self-fueled; to become self-sustained, you must become your own eternal fire lit by your desire to become better every day. What is interesting about individuals is that we all possess the ability to be "great"; in fact, the term "greatness" really relates to the virtues and gifts one possesses. For the warrior, what gives him or her uniqueness is that they possess virtues that are uncommon in the common world. These virtues are accessible to everyone, but few adopt them because they require work, discipline, willpower, faith, and patience. Why are we so enamored by David Blaine, Michael Jordan, Albert Einstein, and Michael Phelps? Well, they attained ultimate mastery over themselves and their gifts, and that is what made them great.

The truth is this: everyone wants success, but they don't want to go through the process of mastering their greatest opponent to achieving success, and that is themselves. Great men and women are remembered for how they were able to exert their will over the direst of situations and how they learned to discipline themselves to achieve, even when they were told it just can't be done. So, you must ask yourself the same question I needed to ask myself: against whom am I competing?

My greatest opponent is myself and my ultimate truth is that time cannot be beaten; Usain Bolt will never actually beat time even if he sets new records. Therefore, maybe the ultimate measure of you, is what you do with the time you have. Maybe it is about how you spend your time and maybe that time should be spent working on improving yourself by strengthening your will. By developing a stronger will over ourselves, every day we can improve and become better and better and better. By strengthening my will I am telling myself that it is ultimately my right to realize my own personal greatness and this is your right to be great, too.

WARRIORS ACCEPT DEATH

Great men and women are remembered not for how they talked but how they acted. It does not matter how exceptional your image is if you lack the wherewithal to execute what it is you want. Great people are remembered because they exercised their will over themselves in the most impossible situations and they accepted death. But the acceptance of death gave them a reason to live.

CHAPTER 8

DEATH AWAKENS THE WARRIOR

"If a warrior is not unattached to life and death, he will be of no use whatsoever. The saying that "All abilities come from one mind" sounds as though it has to do with sentient matters, but it is in fact a matter of being unattached to life and death. With such non-attachment one can accomplish any feat."

— TSUNETOMO YAMAMOTO, HAGAKURE:
THE BOOK OF THE SAMURAI

In my readings of great leaders, I began looking at the life of Martin Luther King, Jr. because he was an elite life athlete. Due to the nature of his cause and the time in which he lived, Martin Luther King, Jr. experienced constant death threats. What Martin understood was that he had to accept the inevitability of death in order for him to live optimally. Living optimally for King meant to live without fear; it

127

meant not being crippled by the fear of death. He knew that accepting death would allow him to perform at his greatest, no matter the situation. In the biography *Martin Luther King, Jr., The Making of a Mind*, it was indicated that King expressed an interest in the existentialist works of Martin Heidegger and was influenced by Heidegger's views on death. Heidegger believed it was the threat of death that provoked authenticity. In Heidegger's view, the larger society's view of death was thought to be inauthentic because we talk as if death is a common occurrence but refuse to believe that we will experience death until it is upon us. We do this to neutralize the threat of death. This is actually supported by a social psychology theory called Terror Management Theory. TMT research supports the view that all human behavior is driven by the fear of our own death.

TMT EXPLAINED

The fact that we have an unconscious awareness that someday we will die is a good thing when it is acknowledged and causes an individual to live their life fearlessly; but it is a problem in most cases because much of our lives are spent seeking the expectations of societal and cultural norms.

TMT explains two concepts about our motivations about death. One factor consists of the individual's notion of the cultural worldview and the confidence one has in this worldview. The second aspect involves a sense of personal value or self-regard that is achieved by accepting as true that one is living up to the cultural system's standards of beliefs. What I mean is that when one is living life outside of fear, it is a good thing, but too many times and for too many people, fear sabotages the ability to optimize life experiences. They simply cannot capitalize on their gifts and talents because they are slaves to their cultures, servants to a false sense of self, and they are robbed of their ability to be all that they can be because they are too afraid to know themselves. They avoid examining their lives to determine if their life direction aligns with their purpose or calling. In effect, they are not motivated by death to live an authentic life; they are motivated by death to die standing on their feet. Socrates stated that the unexamined life is not worth living and Jesus identified the Pharisees as white-washed tombs full of dead men's bones. I believe that we are that way on the exterior; many of us appear to be living lavish lives, but inside we are dead to knowing of ourselves, and this causes us to live dispirited inward lives.

Really what occurs is that one's life becomes unstudied. Decisions and choices are made to appeal to society and are not necessarily based on a clear understanding of who one is and who one is not. The problem is that a lack of questioning one's own personal motivations can create a life that is less than lived. In fact, in coaching sessions, what is very common is to hear clients talk about their beliefs about themselves and life. More times than not, I listen and hear them talk about the fear of not being accepted by family, co-workers, and/or bosses if they choose to take a different direction in their work or life. Sometimes it is just as simple as them owning someone else's idea of who they are.

What I call that is being mastered. Every day we are enslaved by expectations we have adopted as our own by society, race, or political affiliation, and these are the things that can keep you from success in life. Success in life comes from being authentic. A warrior is authentic and warriors that display acts of heroism do it out of a genuine desire to be so.

So, let me ask you a question: if you were to die tomorrow, would the choices you are struggling with today be so hard to make? Probably not. If you were determining whether to make a decision about changing your direction in life, would you make the change knowing that in a week you were going to die? Most likely you would.

You would not care about social norms, the voice of your boss, or even condemnation. You would not be crippled by fear because it wouldn't matter at that point. Which means you would seek to fulfill your full potential because death would motivate you to savor life.

LIBERATION THROUGH ACCEPTANCE

Accepting death is the key to liberating ourselves. It is the key to living an authentic life. How else could Dr. King have been able to do what he did? How else could he accept death without flinching? To understand Dr. King's thinking is to understand the philosophy of the warrior within.

Now think about this for a second: Martin Luther King, Jr. experienced death threats, but regardless of that he optimized life's opportunities anyway and made a social problem his cause to solve. I honestly do not see much difference between him and you. He was human, and you are human. He died, and you will die. King accepted this simple truth and made the choice to leave a legacy. Maybe the comparison is not the same, but actually it boils down to how we choose to spend the time that we have. They say where we choose to place our money is where our heart is. But really it is what we choose to expend our energies; in doing that determines our priorities and often develops our potentials or keeps them from being actualized. I want you to remember this when you think about where to place your energies. In a conversation about wealth, Cyrus the Great said to Croesus, "You realize you cannot eat more than your stomach can hold, and you cannot wear all your gold garments all at once. If you were to try, you would be crushed under the weight of them."

I believe that many of us are crushed under the weight of useless thinking, needless material pursuits that don't bring lasting happiness, and a sense of powerlessness to change things; and it is largely because we have never asked ourselves what would we do differently if tomorrow were the last day we had to live. We simply don't live with the end in mind. Warriors recognize that death is a motivator to live life.

DEATH AS A LIFE MOTIVATION

As morbid as it may seem, the acceptance of death is really a motivator to live. In many ways, it is a means of improving our outlook on life. In psychology we have different reasons for supporting this; in fact, death as a motivator to live can be identified in cases of individuals who have experienced a positive change in themselves and their lives because of a life-altering experience. It's called a Post-Traumatic Growth, and what this refers to is when a person endures a life-threatening situation that changes or alters the way they view life. The outlook of the person changes to reflect life in a more positive light and they focus less on external rewards and more on intrinsic pursuits.

There are hundreds of stories of individuals who have survived near-death experiences that caused them to change their perspective. If an event causes a change of perspective, then is it the event that is the reason for the change or is it the individuals deciding to make a conscious change in themselves? See, a person has the opportunity to change themselves or change their behaviors at any point. It may not be easy, but it is achievable. The reason many individuals don't make changes in their lives is simply because they are conditioned to believe they cannot change through their own beliefs, and even worse, they live in a state of fear. It is more comfortable to stay chained to unrealistic ideas, unhealthy beliefs, toxic people, and useless traditions than to free oneself from mental bondage to the irrational fears residing in the mind. Honestly, it is the elephant in the room.

ELEPHANT SYMBOLISM

Since we are using the elephant analogy, I want to tell you a story about elephants. Now, this was told to me and I want to tell it to you. This has everything to do with the power of the "spirit" and how a mind can be broken by breaking the will or crushing it. The breaking of the will is what happens to the elephants you see in a circus doing tricks for you: they stand on one foot, and even jump through rings of fire. I remember seeing them perform as a child and loved every minute of it. Except even then, I felt sad for them. As a kid I did not know that a baby elephant goes through a process called Phajaan or Crushing in the U.S.; this is a process where they are beaten relentlessly for weeks, starved, their limbs are stretched, and they are chained. Bull hooks are used to stab the head of the animal and pull their ears. This is all done to break the animal's spirit so that it will do as it is told and respond to the trainer's commands. Honestly, it is a nasty business and one I actually am sad I contributed to by going to support the circus, but then, I was only six. After this process is completed, the animal is then passed on to its handler and this person is viewed as the animal's savior. The interesting thing about the process is that the animal's spirit is broken, and they lose the will to fight and they forget how to escape.

Elephants are massive, powerful, intelligent, and emotional creatures. When put under extreme pressure and kept in a sustained state of fear and trauma, their mindsets are altered, their spirits are broken, and they no longer see a way out of their circumstances. Even when the physical shackles are removed from the ankles of the elephant, they are still chained to the memory of the experience. They forget who they are, they forget their strength, they forget they are powerful, and they forget they can overcome. They are dominated by a handler who is smaller in stature and less physically powerful then

132

they are. So, maybe it's not about strength, power, or size and more about having heart, maybe it's about possessing an indomitable will to overcome fear and living for a higher purpose.

We are not captive elephants but when we give into fear, we willingly give our power away to a person, idea, situation, or emotion that does nothing more than weaken our spirit. Ask yourself: are you being mastered by your past? Are you captive to your thoughts? Are you living an optimal life or are you wasting time by living in a past that you cannot change? Are you a victim to the spirit of fear?

THE WARRIOR LEARNS TO RESPOND TO FEAR

What is true is that in order to deal with the issue of death, many times we seek solitude in the confines of a particular culture or group that will give us a sense of identity, and we reinforce this by striving to live up to the expectations of a particular group, social, economic, racial, religious, norm based on the group with which we are affiliated. This feeling of acceptance provides us with a sense of meaning and allows us to disengage from the inevitability of our mortality or finiteness. Truthfully people experience the fear of dying while they are living and that is what confronts them when they are at the end of their lives. They are bombarded with regrets and they wonder if they made the right life choices. But when you think about one's ability to make choices and decisions, you begin to recognize that this is a mechanism that motivates human performance.

Fear, or the "cowardly mind," is what hampers performance for the warrior and it is the dancing elephant in the room that many of us feel we can't stop. In reality, there are two elephants: one is death and the other is fear. What is it about fear much like death that cripples our ability to walk forward, crawl forward, or stop many people dead in their tracks? Well, let's look at the biological basis for fear. Now a minute ago, we discussed the power of confronting death, but most of us avoid the internal dialogue required to accept death for fear of confronting ourselves. Okay, so fear and death go hand-in-hand. So maybe we begin the discussion by talking about elephant number two, the elephant of fear that we choose not to acknowledge. He is dancing right beside you, so let's decide today that we will focus on confronting him by understanding the nature of our fear, or "the spirit of fear."

THE SPIRIT OF FEAR

In order to know the spirit of "fear" and master fear better, let's explain the biological basis of fear; then I will identify what unhealthy fear is, and lastly how it impairs performance. Now first of all, death and fear are ingrained in our human nature. As a warrior, we respect the power of nature, but it is our goal to never give into our own human nature. So, accepting the inevitableness of death and understanding the nature of our own personal fear have to be our goals, or death and fear avoidance will inhibit our overall life performance. Musashi stated that a warrior must "strive for inner judgement and an understanding of everything".

The best thing to start understanding is what triggers your fear, worry, anxiety, and while the mechanism for experiencing fear resides within, it is important to understand that (1) the fear response is a natural response to danger and (2) is a survival mechanism that has assisted the warrior in surviving for centuries. (3) The fear response can also be an unhealthy response that leads to anxiety. (4) Stress, worry, and fear can be triggered by a past experience that hampers your ability to live in the present, and (5) lastly fear does inhibit mental and physical performance, making it difficult to live, work, and thrive. While these concepts are important, recognize that you must become aware of which one motivates your life most heavily.

Fear is a primordial instinct that has been with us since the beginning of time. While it depends upon your view of creation – for instance, the Bible shows fear entering the world when Adam and Eve rebelled against God and evolutionary theory finds it to be a part of our human nature as a survival response required to avoid harm – it is a part of who you are. In any event, it is a biological response to fear or danger. Fear is linked to stress, anxiety, worry, and a host of other issues.

The process of identifying danger is regulated by the amygdala. The amygdala is the brain's central processing center. Its purpose is to relay bits of information and it is like a little alarm that prepares your body to respond to a threat or danger. The amygdala is the primary response mechanism that allows you to assess the threat of a particular situation.

UNHEALTHY FEAR

Fear triggered by the amygdala is expressed at increasing levels as worry, anxiety, terror, and panic. These levels are determined by the imminence of danger. We can become startled and that is a response to an immediate danger; this expresses itself as the fight, flight, or freeze response and originates in the amygdala in the mid-brain. It is triggered when we sense danger. Worry and anxiety are triggered by the anticipation of being harmed in the future. Dread, terror, and panic concern the immediate present.

At the highest levels, terror and panic overwhelm people, causing them to make irrational choices. While terror is an apprehension of impending danger, horror is a sickening and painful experience. Horror is the emotion that lays the foundations for the amygdala to sense the backgrounds of painful events. The amygdala remembers the images, sounds, words and situations that accompanied the horror of injury, ridicule, social rejection, loss of loved ones, or career failure. Subsequently the detection of any related signals trigger fear, often without the person knowing the cause of the fear.

FEAR TRIGGERED BY MEMORIES

When you experience a situation that caused you fear, anxiety, or worry, the brain naturally archives the event in your long-term memory so that it can be recalled, in case a future situation occurs. That is why a fear can cause you to not want to move forward toward making a change in your life. Your body remembers the emotion and reminds you that that situation caused you physical or emotional pain and you don't want nor need to feel that way again, so don't go down that road. Horror is the emotion that lays the foundation for the amygdala to sense the backgrounds of painful events.

FEAR IN THE SHAPE OF WORRY

Worry is frequently based on irrational or unreasonable expectations about the future. This may come from a sense of not knowing how the future will play out, or we feel a sense of instability in our lives. Fear in the shape of worry is always focused around the uncertainty of the future.

FEAR BASED ON IRRATIONAL BELIEFS

Irrational beliefs and unreasonable expectations hijack our higher brain, the prefrontal cortex, which is the seat of judgment and executive functioning. Many of our beliefs were formed so early in childhood that they seem like facts, like a part of who we are. Others were adopted later through cultural influences. Challenging or changing these beliefs may bring up more fears and resistance. We are familiar with the way we think and experience and do not know what our world would be like if we changed our beliefs. This type of fear occurs from not being able to let go of things we learned or were programmed to believe based on what we were taught in our youth.

HOW TO MANAGE A FEAR

To manage fear you must learn to control how you respond to fear. Managing fear requires managing your autonomic nervous system. Your autonomic nervous system regulates your major vital organs. It consists of both your sympathetic and parasympathetic nervous systems. These two systems work together to create homeostasis or balance within your body. The sympathetic nervous system is responsible for the flight or fight and the parasympathetic nervous system is responsible for calming the body down.

To control fear you must learn to control your breathing. When you learn to control your breathing you switch off the sympathetic nervous system and cause the body to calm down.

Try this breathing exercise used by the Navy SEALs to induce the parasympathetic nervous system when confronted with a highly stressful situation that induces the fear state caused by the sympathetic nervous system.

This technique, known as combat or tactical breathing, is an excellent way to reduce your stress and calm down. This breathing strategy has been used by first responders, the military and athletes to focus, gain control and manage stress. In addition, it appears to help control worry and nervousness.

Relax yourself by taking 3 to 5 breaths as described below. Visualize each number as you count.

Breathe in counting 1, 2, 3, 4 Stop and hold your breath counting 1, 2, 3, 4 Exhale counting 1, 2, 3, 4

Repeat the breathing

Breath in counting 1, 2, 3, 4 Pause and hold your breath counting 1, 2, 3, 4 Exhale counting 1, 2, 3, 4

CHAPTER 9

THE WARRIOR LEARNS TO BE COURAGEOUS

"He who conquers himself is the mightiest warrior."
—CONFUCIUS

Did you know that courage is the opposite of fear? In fact, courage is defined as "strength in the face of fear." I often tell my clients that they can be afraid, but they should never give into fear, because fear impedes the warrior's ability to perform. Nelson Mandela expressed his understanding of courage in his autobiography *Long Walk to Freedom* this way: "I have learned that courage was not the absence of fear but triumph over it... the brave man is not he who does not feel fear but he who conquers that fear". If you want to overcome fear it is time that you recognize your fear and then confront it. At the heart of fear is you. What do you fear? What is holding you back from greatness?

TO CONFRONT FEAR MEANS CONFRONTING YOURSELF

As a leader, entrepreneur, or meaning-seeker, you cannot expect to reach your highest potential if your mind is clouded by fear and you are walking in shadows. Nor can one experience or truly understand life's path if s/he lacks the ability to see the shadows of one's own self. In the field of psychology, this is called shadow boxing. A shadow is an aspect of the separate self-story that, for whatever reason, gets repressed and then projected outward as an "other." The "other" is really a reflection of the separate self. We box and hug shadows. To box a shadow is to repress a negative trait and then experience a strong aversion towards others who possess that trait. Aversion is a strong dislike for someone who reminds us of what we do not like about ourselves. They are like a mirror that reflects and reminds us of who we really are. Aversion leads to avoidance. What we do not like in others is what we do not like in ourselves, but fear is what keeps us from confronting the things we do not like within ourselves.

The reality is that it is frightening to confront the darker truths about ourselves. But this is essential to becoming the warrior who is formed from within and it takes courage to explore the places in which we hide. But that is where the journey begins. See, your life is shaped by the unconscious thoughts. It is not the surface that scares me in murky water; rather it is what is below the surface. If you dig deep enough, you will find the sea monsters.

What is interesting is that we lock this part of ourselves away and it wreaks havoc on our lives. It is the place of distorted beliefs, it is the place of our fear, and it takes courage to face the dark side of ourselves. If you want to address this aspect of yourself, it requires being fearless and loving yourself enough to confront the sea monsters lying at the bottom within you. It is time to confront them. This is precisely what I had to do.

MY MOST RIDICULOUS FEAR

This is going to sound ridiculous, but much of my life, I had a fear of the Loch Ness Monster. Blame my high school biology class. I have never seen the Loch Ness Monster, but I knew that every time I would be in murky water, I would think, "What if the Loch Ness Monster is in the water?" It was ridiculous, I know it was. Well, guess what? I eventually confronted my fear a few years ago when I went to Scotland. I actually visited Loch Ness to confront this fear. I began to research this childhood fear, and by seeing the place where Nessie may reside or may have resided, I realized that my fear was exaggerated, irrational, and did not make sense. Hey, laugh if you want. But here is the point: clarity comes when you begin to confront the fears that lie inside of you. See, courage and being courageous is not void of fear; in fact, the dictionary defines it as the ability to face the things that scare you. Courage to face yourself doesn't remove the biological basis for fear, but it alleviates irrational fear. Fear of the Loch Ness Monster was irrational, but the courage to face the fear made me courageous. A warrior is not really invincible, but what makes them perform under pressure is that they are willing to live courageously and face their fears with an immovable mind. I have spent much of my life seeking to overcome the fears that reside within me and it requires daily self-work and constant renewal, or Renovatio.

What you will find is that taking your own path hurts, it's scary, and requires a different spirit. I guess if it were easy, everyone would do it. Many times, the road you are on will be completely opposite of the general population and you will be misunderstood. But being a warrior is an actual way of life. I am often reminded of a Bible passage I read as a boy; I never really understood the context of it then, but I understand it now. (Because the Bible is full of stories of warriors on the path of warriorship, it speaks to me.) Well, I was reading about a certain person named Caleb. In the story, Caleb is told by God that because he possessed a different spirit, he would enter into the Promised Land. The story goes like this:

The Israelites wander for 40 years in the desert, led by a man named Joshua. Joshua sends spies into a land called Canaan to see what the inhabitants are like. So, they come back and the four spies report. All but Caleb give a bad report; they report how gigantic this group of people is and it makes the Tribes of Israel fearful. Because of this, God becomes angry with the spies for frightening the people, but He is pleased with Caleb because he did not possess a spirit of fear. Caleb possessed a spirit of faith, and because of this, God was pleased with him.

Now this is not about giving you a Bible lesson, but what I want to point out is that the road of warriorship is about possessing a different spirit. To possess a different spirit means to take a different path. Warriors do just this. They dedicate their lives to living impeccably and with fearlessness.

ARE YOU FEARLESS?

For the warrior, being fearless is a requirement and a necessity; in fact, it is just another way of identifying the warrior as brave. I read a book by Francis Chan titled *Forgotten God*; in the book, he discussed the life of a particular woman and caused me to pose this question that I pose to you now, because this, to me, is what symbolizes a fearless spirit. The story of Esther Ann Kim gives you an idea of what I mean by being a warrior who walks with courageous fear. So, here is my question: What happens when material things are stripped from you, and you are left with nothing but your person?

In Chan's *Forgotten God*, Esther was placed in a Japanese prison for refusal to worship at Japanese shrines during WWII. Being a devout Christian, this was against her religious beliefs and she chose to spend six years in prison because of her desire to defend her faith. What was so powerful about her story, Chan stated, was to prepare she began developing herself physically, mentally, and spiritually.

> *"To prepare for the fight of her life, each day she would eat decaying food because that was what she would consume in prison. She also spent time reciting and memorizing Bible hymns because she would not be allowed to read her Bible in prison. She would spend time in prayer, preparing her mind to accept that she would be pushed to her limit."*
>
> **FORGOTTEN GOD**

When material things are stripped from us, we must be prepared to rise to the occasion and tap into our greatest potentials that can only be found inside of us, and through a recognition that life's purpose is not found in what we acquire but by the path we commit to, what we are willing to fight for, and what we are willing to let go of. What we put our faith in will either sustain us or destroy us. To achieve greatness requires everything in us, the support of those close to you, and always a deep faith in God's ability to direct our path. Even the warrior understands that faith in oneself is limited, and when faith in ourselves is lacking, faith in a higher purpose will guide us to reach our greatest potentials. The spirit is limitless, and the power of God is boundless, and that is what He has placed within us. When our personal power is connected to a spiritual force we can survive, we can suffer and even give ourselves whole-souled to something or someone, and in the midst of the crisis find peace. For the warrior, life is about acquiring and maintaining the personal power within oneself.

When you do not strengthen your whole person, you risk giving your power away. Some of us give and have given so much of ourselves away that we do not know who we are anymore. Maybe you need to renew your spirit and reclaim what you have lost.

WHAT DID VIKTOR FRANKL EXPERIENCE?

To really understand the true nature of power and faith in the human spirit, the account of Viktor Frankl's life clearly describes in detail the power of the human spirit and the importance of meaning. In fact, his book was the book that inspired me to go deeper into understanding purpose.

His story marked the beginning of my personal Renovatio, or desire to renew my life, some 14 years ago. I think I picked up his book in 2007 when I was in the library at Webster University. I do not remember how exactly I came across his work. No matter, the power of his story spoke to my spirit. He brought me to tears and gave me a sense of hope; the realism of his work rocked my soul.

I felt a similar feeling the first time I read a book called *Night* by the late author, Elie Weisel. That book touched me deeply as a younger man, but Frankl's *Man's Search for Meaning* has forever changed me. See, there is power in a story. Viktor Frankl was an author and psychiatrist, and is widely known for this book, which he wrote while in a concentration camp in Auschwitz, Germany. There he endured hunger, being stripped to nakedness; and even in the state of nothingness, Frankl determined that no matter the situation, one can still be free to choose an attitude or disposition. Even in the direst of circumstances, one can wield power over how s/he deals with a given situation or circumstance. In fact, Frankl wrote *Man's Search for Meaning* while in the concentration camps from an observational perspective. What is remarkable about Frankl is that he utilized his environment as a means to practice self-reflective behaviors and be present. He used his life as a laboratory and it allowed him to grow by optimizing the challenges presented through life in the concentration camps. He did not give into despair and lose hope in a better tomorrow, even though he had been a prisoner in three different concentration camps and even though he lost his wife and children. While he could not avoid the harsh realities of the concentration camps, he understood his resolve and was determined. He describes how he approached the challenges of his life and exercised personal power over his particular situation:

> *"Even though conditions such as lack of sleep, insufficient food, and various mental stresses may suggest that the inmates were bound to react in certain ways, in the final analysis it becomes clear that the sort of person the prisoner became was the result of an inner decision, and not the result of camp influences alone. Fundamentally, therefore, any man can, even under such circumstances, decide what shall become of him — mentally and spiritually."*

Life is a striving to fulfill a purpose. Here is the reality: purpose is a spiritual aspect of who you are. Every one of us seeks to find the purpose, but to do this, a certain amount of whole person power is required to experience the Will to Meaning for the warrior. When the warrior is able to accept particular conditions and choose to maintain composure by keeping his mind, body, and spirit intact, a warrior develops an attitude of immovability and possesses an unfettered mind. This is the demonstration of personal power and gives way to a strengthened resolve.

It is the strength within you that will help you to arrive at your vision. The ability to exhibit personal power opens the door for the warrior to find his/her will to meaning and exert a will to personal power. The will to meaning is the natural tendency of each human being to seek a purpose for life. This is your right and it is available to you right now. So, what is your vision for your life? And what are you doing today to arrive at it?

One more thing: even in a place of confinement, Frankl was able to write his greatest work. His purpose was stronger than prison. How strong is your purpose, and more importantly, has it become the vision for which you live?

What do you want people to say about you at your funeral?

Imagine that you passed away many, many years from now. Write whatever comes to mind. Take 10-15 minutes to complete this exercise. Questions you should ask yourself as you do this exercise:

- What and/or who did you impact or change? Why?

- What character traits and values did you consistently demonstrate over your life? At your core, who were you?

- Who did you care for? How did you impact or change this person/these people?

- What were major accomplishments in your life? At the ages of 40, 50, 60, 70?

- What did you show interest in? What were you passionate or enthusiastic about?

- What was your legacy?

The only thing worse than being blind
is having sight but no vision.

— HELEN KELLER

WARRIORS SEEK THE VISION

Vision is the blueprint of a warrior's strategy.

The great warrior Miyamoto Musashi believed that achieving the spirit of the warrior required understanding strategy. He stated, "Study strategy over the years and achieve the spirit of the warrior. Today is victory over yourself of yesterday; tomorrow is your victory over lesser men."

If you have ever experienced a plateau, or if you are feeling stuck in your life, then it is likely that you lack a vision for your life.

What is important to understand about life is that life without vision is not life at all. For the warrior, a clear vision is a strategic road map for life.

In fact, Musashi understood firsthand the problem that arises when you do not plan and be mindful of your day-to-day interactions. A lack of vision derails performance; that is why you can never underestimate the power of a clearly crafted strategy, and it is always good to be in prayer about your life direction. Similarly, tapping your human potential and mastering your work or life pursuits is a matter of continuous, persistent effort and essential to developing the warrior mindset. To achieve a high level of performance requires understanding yourself as a person and fulfilling your innate programming of being goal-directed.

Much of your life will have to be driven by the pursuit to excel in the field you have chosen to master, and progress will be slow, and the road will be difficult. Musashi identified these truths in his famed *Book of Five Rings*. He stated that:

1. "The attainment of mastery is an endless process that one will spend a lifetime seeking to grasp."
2. "The importance of developing strategy is what will allow you to overcome obstacles in your life." In fact, he suggested that thinking and living strategically is essential to becoming a warrior.
3. But most importantly he stated that it takes passion, patience, and self-discipline to take the journey.

Musashi understood well the importance of strategy or proper planning. Indeed, in his later life, his lack of self-understanding led him to a place of questioning, and questioning led to sojourning in a cave. No matter how successful you become, at some point you will find yourself again in a state of obscurity. In the beginning, you may be unknown to the world; but in the end, if you do not work on yourself, you will be unknown to yourself and your potential. You can have it all, but if you have not addressed the existential questions in your life, you will find yourself sojourning in a cave too.

I am inclined to believe that this is what happened to Musashi. He achieved expert performance but lost purpose. Born in 1584 in Mimasaka, Japan, Musashi was known for being highly skilled in combat. It is recorded that he won his first duel at the age of thirteen and later became a ronin (masterless samurai). He is known for inventing the style of fencing with two swords, and was renowned for fighting in more than sixty duels. But for all Musashi's accomplishments in war, he realized a truth about his existence: he did not understand the strategic nature with which he was able to overcome his opponents. Though he achieved great success in his life, he did not understand himself.

In retrospect, to not understand himself meant having a limited understanding of his gifts, abilities, and human performance. He did not spend time recording how he achieved greatness.

See, Musashi could not identify what was the basis for his great success and superior ability. From ages thirteen to twenty-nine, Musashi developed impeccable skill in the art of combat but found himself puzzled by the nature of his performance. He lived and acted instinctively. At the age of sixty, the need to contemplate and understand the nature of his superior performance compelled him to take a different path. The desire to address this void within himself caused him to sojourn in a cave. His desire to uncover the way of strategy was so impelling that he retired to a cave called the Reigan

Cave to contemplate the nature of his performance, which would later become The *Book of Five Rings*. While Musashi discusses his way of strategy in The *Book of Five Rings*, what he likely did not expect on this journey of self-reflection was to find peace and ultimately find at the heart of strategy a deeper understanding of himself.

See, even a spirit at war can find peace, and it comes through contemplation and seeking to understand the purpose of one's life. For a man who fought from age thirteen to twenty-nine, it is likely he may have lost a piece of himself.

Now, I do not glorify the art of killing, but what can be learned from Musashi is that the path of a warrior revolves around developing a growth mindset required to master a skill. Also it is important to recognize that, for all of his valor, he could not cheat the inevitability of death. It did not matter how skilled he was; every warrior must accept the inevitability of death. Because it is the one certainty that can be predicted. You and I cannot know the day we will die, but we can be confident that it can and will happen. This is just a reality. So, what are you doing with your time? Do you seek to understand the great gifts that reside within you? Do you focus on developing self-mastery? To understand the totality of your life requires identifying your purpose and crafting a vision.

YOU CAN DESIGN THE LIFE YOU WANT

Purpose is found through setting goals, assessing yourself, and envisioning. One of the most powerful books I have ever read on the topic of self-management was written by Zingerman's Deli owner Ari Weinzweig, titled Managing Ourselves. Ari speaks about how self-management has been a major factor in his public and private life. But what I most know him for is his emphasis on envisioning. In his book, Ari makes a distinction between envisioning and just daydreaming. He stated, "Daydreaming can be delicious, but it rarely changes reality."

This is pretty profound on many levels. What this means is that one can live passively but vision is an active experience. Daydreamers do not pursue dreams; they are pacifists, ever chasing but never catching their dreams because dreams are illusive. Visions, however, are kinetic pursuits lived in the realm of possibility and acted on realistically. They are fueled by those who say, "I can," "I will," "I must," and "I will do." Visionaries assimilate a dream from a state of dreaming to an ideal, and from an ideal to a vision, and from a vision to a living reality. Such is the nature of the warrior: he utilize visions as mental blueprints to establish an endpoint or destination. In Mihaly's book on creativity, he describes the creative process as follows:

PREPARATION

During this phase, you are wrestling with a problem that you seek to solve. See, you have become aware of something and it has begun to take hold in your mind. I believe the highest form of envisioning comes from aligning your gifts and talents with a higher purpose, or when it is directed at a social problem that needs to be resolved. For instance, I have a client who has a passion for fitness and his vision is to decrease obesity and bullying around the world. Because he has become uniquely aware of his talents and gifts, he has been able to align them with a career that focuses on improving social issues. But he had to sit and think about what he really wanted to change in life.

Here is my question for you: what social issue have you identified or what problem exists that you feel you could commit your life to? You will know it when you see that one thing that continually jerks at your heart and stays on your mind.

INCUBATION

During the stage of incubation, you are really seeking to connect the dots between purpose, passion, and possible linkages. When I was doing my dissertation, I wanted to understand the relationship between servant leadership, work meaning, life meaning, and employee engagement. On the surface, it seemed as though they did not connect, but as I let the idea evolve over a period of time that I spent reading different literature, I began to see connections between the concepts. But it was difficult to know how they were all related. One thing about life and problem solving is that they are a creative endeavor. While linkages may not seem like they exist between two concepts or ideas, if you dig hard enough you will begin to see that linkages do in fact exist.

INSIGHT

When you assess your life for purpose, a clear indication of what you are supposed to do will come in the form of a new understanding. I began to recognize my life purpose as I journaled over time. But what gave me clarity was that I became mindful of reinforcing moments. Reinforcing moments are moments that represent what I told you about earlier. These are those moments or interactions that you have experienced over the course of your life that inform your life direction.

For me, as a boy, I always wanted to help someone. I loved to support, to listen, and to encourage individuals. A funny thing about me is that I remember at the age of seven being asked what I wanted to do with my life. I told my mother I wanted to become a flower man because they made people happy. Now I know that that might be a stupid thing to say, but hey, I was a child and it looked like a pretty good gig. Although I never became a flower man, a lot of what I do revolves around helping individuals find something beautiful within them. See, your purpose is not apparent right away; it matures as you experience life, work, and moments of solitude, but you will see hints of what you love by observing yourself and thinking of the moments that bring you the greatest joy.

EVALUATION

The evaluation stage is likely the most daunting because at this stage, you have to lock down exactly what it is you want out of life and begin moving toward making it a reality. So, this is where you have to determine if this vision is worth the effort. I have found that the period of evaluation can be a trying time because during the evaluation period, you don't truly know what the full expectations are, and you do not know just how committed you will have to be to achieve your vision. Some people never leave the stage of evaluation. But honestly, you cannot know unless you get on with the experience.

ELABORATION

Once you have come to the stage of elaboration, you now have to make that idea into a physical reality. This is the stage where most people quit. They get on the road to renewal but find it hard to stay there because it is far easier to dream and talk about what you want, but it is a fight to actually achieve what you want. Oftentimes, when pursuing a vision for your life, you will have to pick yourself up from setbacks. You may have to look at your vision as means to remind you of the journey that you are on.

HAVE YOU EVEN WRITTEN DOWN YOUR VISION?

Ari Weinzweig, is an authority on the practice of envisioning and advocates the importance of vision casting. He suggests that everyone write a vision statement because it helps to define where one is going in life and increases the likelihood of getting there. Ari is correct: envisioning is important in work and life, but he recognizes that it is rarely done in our modern society and that is why he travels the country, teaching how to do it. This is essential for a meaning-seeker, a warrior, a leader, an entrepreneur, or just an average everyday person. Really, a vision is one way to explore personal truth and reclaim personal power. I am not talking about the ultimate truth; I am talking about the truth as a personally powerful kind of truth: the truth about who you are and what you fear. In fact, Ari stated "a significant number know that writing a vision is the right thing to do, but they're a bit afraid of what might come out when they put their future down on paper".

I believe that a fear of recording one's vison has everything to do with the fast-paced nature of life and the downright fear of the future that most people feel. To write a vision requires slowing down; it requires sitting, being quiet, and listening to the voice in your head. People would rather speed forward than have to sit quietly and determine what they really want in life. To sit would mean having to confront the reality of life. You know what I mean: am I really happy doing what I am doing? Do I find fulfillment in life or am I pretending? In Western society, college is a way to avoid the reality of life, or we wait till a crisis occurs in our lives that forces us to think about the age-old questions: "Who am I, what am doing here, and what is my purpose?"

In an interview with Dan Millman, in The Awakened Warrior, he states:

> "Many people are frustrated they haven't had a coming-of-age, male or female. They say, 'Okay, so now you're an adult.' But how do they know? One very important part of education is really testing youngsters, putting stretch marks on their souls, letting them see they can go beyond what they think they can do, like they did in many native societies. People need to see the warrior, the power. People need to face their own moment of truth".

Perhaps the problem with modern society is that we do not truly have a definitive idea of rites of passage and young men and women are not taught how to seek a vision for their lives. They do not have an idea of how powerful their bodies, minds, and spirits are because they have never been tested. The only arenas that are left that test us are sports. I think Ari is right: a deficient vision comes from not being taught how to be a visionary. We are not taught to sit, to wait, or to listen with spiritual discernment. Our bodies have not been pushed to a breaking point; we are not reared to seek out discomfort. Rather, we are taught

155

to seek out pleasure and mistake it as purpose. We choose professions based on how they can fulfill our desire for security, but rarely do we actually take the time to determine how the work we do makes us feel. We disengage from that, but we are always asking ourselves if what we do is making a difference.

The 21st century is proving that work is not a way to find completion. The reason is that work is one aspect of life's totality, but it does not provide ultimate meaning; it merely offers a sense of meaning for some and meaninglessness for most. We are taught to go to school, find a job, get married, and towards the end of your life, reflect on what you should have done differently. This leaves many of us feeling empty and powerless with a bucket list we will never get to, because we are too busy daydreaming and not actively pursuing the true purpose for our lives. We do not know what we are capable of because we have not tested our limits. To not test your limits and learn to go beyond just being basic renders you powerless to your life and you cannot achieve ultimate mastery that way.

WHY YOU FEEL POWERLESS

The feelings of powerlessness come from feeling like there is no control of one's life. The reality is you give your personal power away every time you avoid thinking about what you really want in your life. You make yourself powerless every time you look to the past for purpose. You give your power away every time you say I am trying, every time you compromise your values, and every time you do not accept responsibility for your choices. You become powerless when you fail to recognize that you are both your jailor and the jail cell. If you are both, that means powerlessness can be reversed when you flip your thinking and realize you have the key to changing your life; but you have to find the place you dropped the key to freedom, and that is usually somewhere in your past. You have either given your power away to a person, place, or thing and it usually causes you to question the identity of your person. Pick up the key, unlock the prison of your thoughts, and leave the past where it belongs: in the past. No past will ever be greater than the promise of the future; the past is not better than the potential for a beautiful future. The past is merely a daydream. You can't change what has already occurred, but you can craft a vision for a new you and a new life. This is the way of the warrior within.

LEAVE THE PAST IN THE PAST

In my coaching sessions, I always listen to clients reflect on the past. The conversations focus on "what I should have done" but I always ask, "Did you possess the personal resources to change that situation then, to what you feel it should be now?" The answer is usually, "No, I was not thinking then the way I think now." The past must stay in the past, I say, but you can do something about today; you can do something about right now.

So, what are you going to do about it? When a client reflects on the past, I view these as daydreams because a past does not direct the future; a compelling vision does. OK, then, where are you at with your vision? Are you working to make it a reality or are you experiencing the winkle syndrome? (You will understand that in a minute. Just keep reading.) I often think to myself: what will happen when they finally wake up?

See, what you may not realize is that when you look to the past to grow your future, you are really not moving at all. Let me tell you a story I used to love as a kid – yes, I am going back to the past, but I am going back because it is relevant to the journey we are on.

THE WINKLE EFFECT

As a boy, I remember reading a story by Washington Irving. He was an American writer who wrote short stories that we used to listen to during story time at Jonas Salk School.

The story goes like this: there was a man named Rip Van Winkle who lived on the edge of the Catskills Mountains in a small little town. He was the kind of guy who would always duck responsibility. See, Rip had this wife who nagged him all day long to work. Rip, of course, just didn't have a vision for that sort of thing. He enjoyed stealing away to nap, hunting in the woods, drinking moonshine... he loved to explore pleasure because that was what he believed made him happy. Apparently, he was a master napper. (You know that person who could sleep in any situation, under any conditions, and he was dedicated to sleep time.)

Anyway, one day Rip goes off into the forest because he hears loud, striking thunder. Well, it turns out these little bearded dwarves are playing a game of nine pins. So, Rip decides to hang out with them and gets comfortable, drinks some of their moonshine. He falls asleep, and when he wakes up, the whole world has changed. He begins to notice that he has aged and life as he knows it has changed. He goes to find his family and they don't recognize him. When he sees his daughter, she is an adult and has children of her own. Rip realizes he slept for thirty years.

My point is, warriors do not sleepwalk; they know they are awake and live each day with the end in mind.

TIME-BOUND BUT NOT BOUND TO A PARTICULAR TIME

A warrior is conscious of time and understands and acknowledges that time is a valuable commodity that must not be wasted. In essence, time is viewed as being important; and as such, it is important to set goals that are time-bound. But the warrior recognizes that time is a continuum where the past, present, and future exist in coalescence. You don't have time to waste because it is limited.

See, the search for a beginning starts for the warrior by seeking the meaning or purpose for his or her life. I call this living with the end in mind. Don't waste your time on things that possess no meaning or do not fit with your journey; they will only take your vitality.

Honestly, what happens when the daydream passes, and we recognize our pursuits were not legacy-building pursuits? What happens when you have aimed so small and you leave so little of yourself behind that you are forgotten? What happens when you have given all of yourself to something that is not you? You will say to yourself, "I haven't even started yet."

See, the Catch-22 about our lives is they are finite, and it takes time to build everything if you want to be anything. Legacies are built over time, through sweat, toil, and goal-directedness. They are not built on living in the past. Warriors choose where to put their physical, mental, emotional, and spiritual energies, and they choose how they want to spend their time. So, why do we not want to accept that the time we put in yields the fruit appropriate to our labor?

When you focus on building a legacy you will be remembered; but when your focus is on making life all about pleasure, you will yield a return on that time too. What happens is this: when you finally wake up, you realize you wasted the most precious commodity you have, the greatest gift under heaven: your time to develop self-mastery so you can achieve skill-mastery.

Don't Rob Yourself of Time

The greatest killer of performance is wasting time on anti-mastery activities.

What are you wasting time on?

How are these anti-mastery activities keeping you from the better version of yourself?

What do you need to be doing that will get you closer to your vision for your life?

PART 3
SELF-MASTERY – GIFTEDNESS

CHAPTER 10

FROM FEAR TO POWER

"Don't pray for an easy life. Pray for the strength to endure a difficult one."
— BRUCE LEE

Please review my story again. Notice how my perspective has changed. Notice how I have transitioned from a place of pain to a place of power. I did it by choosing to see the past as a teaching lesson. I changed the story I was telling myself. How can you do the same in your life?

Being a warrior requires us to submerge ourselves in the ocean of our fears, only to find that we have the ability to rise back to the top more renewed. Every time we face our fears, we are given new breath. A feeling of powerlessness is merely a feeling; it is merely an experience at a particular time in your life, but it is never forever. My early life is a testament to that fact.

See, I remember with vividness at the age of three being brought to Chicago, Illinois from Arkansas with my brothers and sisters. What is peculiar about that situation is this: I started life in a pair of little girl's underwear and a ripped-up t-shirt. I remember us being separated by different family members, and I remember the first time I opened a pantry full of food and being amazed that so much food existed in a house. I remember being too afraid to ask for food, and so I would hide in the closet and eat the food. The thing was, I did not have to. But I had to unlearn this habit and I also had to accept that past experiences did not determine my future and they were not my only certainty. What was far more important from the struggles in early life was utilizing them as emotional motivation to do more, be more, and achieve more. That is why you have to learn from setbacks, use them as a motivation to press forward, and find pleasure in struggle, because in struggle you find purpose. Embrace pain. It is a reality of life and in all honesty it is a necessity. One more thing: you are only as powerless or as powerful as you allow yourself to be. Miyamoto Musashi stated this about becoming a warrior:

"Do not sleep under a roof. Carry no money or food. Go alone to places frightening to the common brand of men. Become a criminal of purpose. Be put in jail, and extricate yourself by your own wisdom."

Now, the story of my early life may sound like a sob story, and it may seem as if I was powerless and I am in denial. But the reality is I was not powerless and I have never been powerless. My biggest issue has always been that I possess a very strong will. I will, because I can; I can because I do; and just like me, whatever you have been through, whatever you are going through will make you stronger if you embrace it. This is what it means to build your will-house. At the age of three, I began building my will-house of willpower to prepare me for the vision of my life. I just didn't know it yet. I was being prepared for this moment, to write these words; I was being forged into something more. Understand this:

- I first had to recognize that I may have been powerless to the decisions of others, but I could always empower myself to rise above the difficult experiences because it was not who I was. It was just an experience. I did not have to own it as permanent, but I had to recognize that it was an exercise utilized as a means to strengthen my willpower and learn to leverage it as a means to build personal mastery. Tragic circumstances can be harnessed and used to create elite performance. You must learn to tap into the pain of your experience and use it to fuel your desire for excellence.

- I also had to recognize that to survive was a temporary aim, because life is work and to take the journey means to accept the tension of being where you are in order to get where you want to be. See, the journey as a life-athlete only ends when you die, but your ability to succeed will come from pushing through the pain, all the while managing your perspective. Because nothing lasts forever; it may seem like forever, but nothing lasts forever.

- Most importantly, you must recognize that pain is a requirement for success, or maybe you are the one person in history who never had to learn to crawl as a newborn. You got up and just started walking. No, you came into the world and it was painful; when you began walking you fell, so why not accept that there is gonna be a level of discomfort and get on with it! Every warrior must be tested. Suffering is merely success in disguise.

When you think about life and hard experiences, understand that life's conditioning has not changed throughout history. But it is the secret to success.

Success is not and will never be built on a comfortable life or a predictable situation. It is built on hustle. For whatever reason, comfortable predictability just is not a part of the law of success. Building a strong will and your ability to overcome adversity is what changes realities, it is what changes social consciousness, and it is what takes the warrior from a place of obscurity to being a legend. Because success is a battle of will. Bruce Lee stated that "will makes a man, but success takes perseverance". A study of great warriors and warrior cultures can be compared to what is required of anyone seeking to excel in modern-day life.

I stated that I was in training though I did not know it. Well, it is true. If you review the Spartan culture, you come to recognize that young boys were bred for war and to be indomitable in battle, but the training was harsh and it began at a young age. The Spartan was revered and some believe they were some of the greatest fighters to ever live. In order to become great fighters, the young Spartan males from the age of seven were trained at the Agoge in the arts of fighting, will building, and survival in harsh conditions. Even today, similar practices are utilized to harden a soldier; as a runner we would run in all terrains and in various conditions.

See, the greatest way to improve performance is to increase the mental tension required for one to perform. To forge an indomitable spirit requires being beaten, broken, in order to be rebuilt. Life will naturally do this. Sometimes it is by our own design and it is involuntary and sometimes it is because it's necessary to achieve something. Regardless, being comfortable is not an ingredient for a successful journey. But you can endure almost anything if it is meant for a purpose.

Now, everyone suffers. Everyone has a story, but not everyone is able to see that pain is temporary. Some of us just aren't able to renew our minds. But it is that painful experience that inspires us and teaches us that we are more than what the eyes can see. So be careful who you judge. I always say: you never know what your opponent has under the hood. He may look like he can go one round but he just might take you twelve. One of the reasons for the Renovatio symbol being the impossible triangle is that the triangle is actually a two-dimensional object but the eyes view it in 3D. See, how you perceive something determines your response to it.

If it is experience that drives us to submerge ourselves in the depths of our despair and rise with greater fortitude and more fire, then it is required to build your storehouse of will-power. But again, we have to stop looking at things as forever when the truth is they are temporary. What lasts forever is regret and living with an if kind of L(if)e. Let me tell you that it is a heavy burden to carry, knowing you did not do what you should have done, knowing that you did not give what you could have given, and knowing that you did not say what you should have said. "If" will never allow you to live life fully; it will only leave you wanting more out of your life because "if" does not make you experience the whole of your life. It merely limits your life to a past you cannot live in and keeps you from defining the future.

I placed this quote by Lance Armstrong in my journal some time ago to remind me of this truth. It goes like this:

"Pain is temporary. It may last a minute, or an hour, or a day, or a year, but eventually it will subside and something else will take its place. If I quit, however, it lasts forever. That surrender, even the smallest act of giving up, stays with me. So when I feel like quitting, I ask myself: which would I rather live with?" (Armstrong, It's Not About the Bike: My Journey Back to Life).

FOCUS ON WHAT YOU CAN CONTROL

See, what I have come to learn about my own trials is this: the beginning of my training as a young warrior and the beginning of the forging of my will started from my birth, but I swore that I would eventually rise above the heartache, disappointment, and irrational beliefs. The experience did not and would not be my future because I was meant for more in my life; that was what made that moment with stars so special. Have you ever thought that the setback in your life or your work was merely a means to teach you something? Maybe it was preparing you for a time when you would have to call upon those experiences in order to overcome an insurmountable foe. As I have become older, I am thankful for this experience. I swore to myself that while I could never control the decisions and experiences of others, I could develop mastery over my own mind, body, spirit, and emotions. Elite athletes are taught to focus only on what they control; anything else is a waste of energy.

In running we are taught to be efficient with our energy and not to concentrate on the competitor in the lane next to us. We are taught at a young age to stay in our lanes, keep our knees up, never let up, and P.U.S.H. through the pain no matter what. We were taught to leave it all on the track and waste no time on thinking about what happened in the last race, because it was more important to produce our best effort in the race before us. See, every race is different, every moment is different, and no contest is going to end the same. In the field of competitive sports (for me, it was running), it's important to accept the wins and losses of the past; but it's more important to rebuild, never stay down, and always push forward. Stay in control by continuing to learn and reflect on your life.

Reflective Practice

To develop your ability to focus on what you can control, you must identify the things that you have control over before pursuing a difficult endeavor. What I think you will find is that if you can control your internal state, your outward reality will change.

What aspects of a specific situation can you control?

- You can control your response to the situation.

- You can control how you feel about the situation.

- You can control what you do in the situation.

- You can control how much you think about the situation.

- You can control how you perceive the situation.

- You can prepare for the situation.

- You can anticipate the situation.

- You can choose to learn from the situation.

LEARN TO BECOME POWERFUL

One of the fundamental human needs required of human beings is a desire to feel in control or have a sense of power in their lives. When we are stripped of our sense of power, our lives become meaningless to us. If you feel a sense of powerlessness, it has everything to do with your life perspective. Powerlessness is a construct of a feeling that life has no meaning or purpose. It comes from not feeling like you are living a life of purpose. Well, remember I told you that your emotions can mislead you? Life is full of purpose but a negative mindset cannot see this as truth.

Regardless of what your life or work goal is, to obtain it you must recognize that you are meant to continually learn. Learning is essential to attaining work/life-mastery. Now, the ability to obtain mastery is only acquired through understanding the self and improving learning competency, and to do this really is contingent on being a lifelong student of your chosen craft and a student of yourself.

It is essential that you begin to understand the learning process because both self-mastery and skill-mastery require developing understanding of what is necessary to optimize your full potentials to live a complete and full life. A great way to understand self-mastery is to realize that all mastery is driven by learning to be competent. That means you must learn the process of learning and begin to comprehend how you learn in the process of learning.

MASTERY REQUIRES LEARNING

There are various models of learning. The renovatio meaning-based warrior trajectory really is a competency model much like the Dreyfus competency model; this asserts that to gain mastery one must go through five stages: novice, competence, proficiency, expertise, and then finally mastery. This model is not too different from the model used in the field of Aikido called Shuhari, which proposes that mastery is a three-stage process requiring learning, detaching, and transcending.

All of these learning models identify learning as a process of developing a competency. That means to be successful at business, life, work, or relationships requires learning to be competent.

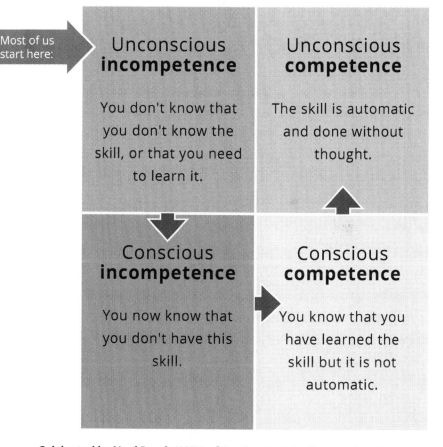

Originated by Noel Burch (1970) of Gordon Training International.

In the beginning of self-development or skill mastery you must first learn the basics of your craft. The problem with the learning process is that you do not know what you do not know. This is why it is important to find a mentor. When you have learned the basics they become automatic or instinctive. This allows you to begin to remove yourself from mental contemplation, which is a time when you have to the think about the process of learning in order to execute a function of action. You are conscious of your incompetence but you are still learning the basics. When you have become aware of what you need to learn the next step is to become competent. When you are able to teach your trade to another then you have arrived at a place of conscious competence. However, what will bring you to the phase of mastery is when you live, think, and act without even thinking about what you are doing. You become one with your knowing. When you have developed your skill and it becomes innate you then begin the process of going beyond the limits of your craft. In my opinion it then becomes creative.

Most of us will never arrive at mastery because we hold on to outdated mental models that provide the necessary structure we need to achieve proficiency of our craft. Structure is important, discipline is important, but at some point your existing mental models will cause you to experience work/life plateaus. The reason for this is that what allowed you to succeed in one phase of work/life mastery does not work in a newer phase of learning and growth. You are adaptive and your learning must be adaptive as well. New growth requires new learning. You must break with social norms and popular mental models if you want to arrive at a new level of success. You must tear down outdated mental models and design new ways of seeing the world in order to arrive at your goals. What worked in the past may be what is holding you back from the future. Learning is fluid, it is ever expanding and this is how you must approach your life because it is the gift of learning that fuels your potential to become the better version of yourself. No matter the learning competency model, if you seek to achieve ultimate life mastery, you must stay the course, listen for the lessons, and execute on your goals with extreme focus and accept that it will take time to achieve your vision. Do not be afraid to try something new. Do not be afraid to fail, because failure is the doorway to success when you are learning how to succeed in life. Stay the course.

CHAPTER 11

STAY THE COURSE

"The journey of a thousand miles begins with one step. "
—LAO TZU

Warriorship is about staying the course. In fact, that was what the great Hannibal Barca stated. Barca was a military commander of the Carthage army. He led a famous campaign in the second Punic War against the Roman army, remaining undefeated until the very gates of Rome. He stated, "We will either find a way or make one."

For you to be victorious, you must stay the course; and when there seems to be no way, you must make one. The reality of work/life performance optimization is that there is always a way and every day you make that way clear through your choices. The road to Renovatio is a deeper journey because it seeks to unify the mind, body, and spirit. It is a road to greater conviction. It is a road that promises to provide intrinsic value because it is a journey of the spirit and ends with learning to optimize every second and every moment of your life, knowing that you are significant and your life is of significance. I remember being told years ago by someone that I was not significant because in their mind they had determined I had never done anything significant in my life. Well, everyone has the ability to judge another, but the reality is we do not know the warrior who stands before us and we do not really know what someone is capable of. All of us are capable of being great, but we have to find that one thing that inspires us to be great. Now, don't get me wrong: at the time I had accomplished many things, but how would he have known? Greatness cannot be judged by another; it can only be determined by you. Do not ever listen to the critics; keep pursuing your goals, regardless of who or what stands in your way.

Barca managed to lead his Carthaginian army over the Alps and into Italy to take the war directly to the Roman Republic. The Alps were a less than ideal route, but what made the act so extraordinary is that he rode into Rome on an elephant. I don't think they saw that coming but Hannibal was a man of strategy. (Honestly, that is strategy if I say so myself.) Even more than that, it represents the measure of a man. He found a way even when it may have seemed like no way existed. See, who can measure a man but the man himself? I love Corinthians 2:11, which says: "For what man knoweth the things of a man, save the spirit of man which is in him? Even so the things of God knoweth no man but the Spirit of God." Dr. Martin Luther King, Jr. said it best when he stated: "The ultimate measure of a man is not where he stands in moments of comfort and convenience, but where he stands at times of challenge and controversy."

To become a warrior is a path that begins now! It begins in every minute and every second of your life. To become a warrior requires finding a direction because warriorship is a path that requires a vision and equates to developing a performance mindset. Warriorship is not like leading others; the difference between the two is that a warrior must first learn to lead him or herself before s/he can lead another. Warriors reflect on their accomplishments only long enough to learn from them. This is important to overcoming obstacles in their paths. Do you continually find yourself making the same mistakes and never learning from them?

While modern-day leadership seeks to lead through the wielding of external power and outward influence, warriors focus on developing their personal power. It is the power of self-control or self-management or self-will that defines the warrior and allows this person to lead from the inside out. Similarly, a warrior seeks a vision because the warrior understands that meaning in life is a spiritual journey requiring it to be viewed from the mind's eye and not the natural eye.

Miyamoto Musashi in The Book of Water expressed it best when he said, "a warrior must learn to see things far away and up close" because "peripheral vision is of the utmost importance; it is a skill that is developed over a period of time in training and in everyday life."

Warriors live and train to perform, to act, to move, to rise to the occasion. While they seek the vision for life, it is important that they take action toward making it real. Mihaly identified optimal experience as times when we feel in control of our actions, masters of our own fate... these moments are viewed as the best moments in our lives not because they were easy, but because they were difficult. Mihaly suggests that these moments are moments when we feel most alive. In these moments we are stretched mentally, physically, emotionally, and spiritually by the complexity of an undertaking; but it is in these moments we find our greatest pleasure. You cannot hope for greatness; you must work towards it, develop a vision for it, and be ready to master yourself if you seek to master your craft. This requires developing a laser focus on your specific area of focus, aligning all your energies toward it, and expecting to be stretched to your breaking point. Living an optimal life requires accepting the challenges of today in order to be stronger tomorrow.

Warriorship is about taking the path that fits you best; I love the story of King David in the Bible. As the story goes, he determined that he would fight the giant Goliath. But what was really interesting about David is that he chose to fight Goliath with a slingshot. When King Saul offered him armor to fight the giant, David rejected the armor of Saul because he recognized his success was not tied to untested armor. Now most men would have gone against this giant with a suit of armor and a sword. But David possessed three stones, a sling, and the word of God. Even when he was laughed at, he stayed the course. Even when people thought he was crazy to go against a giant like Goliath with only a sling and rocks, he persisted on his path of warriorship. What you realize is that David carried a deep conviction for the things of his God, Yahweh, and placed his faith and belief in himself and the Spirit. He did not choose the path that the average man would follow. Instead, he chose the harder road and it only built him into a more indomitable human being, making him immovable in faith. A warrior becomes indomitable when the spirit is forged in accord with the mind and body.

Much like the body, the spirit is essential to living. Now, you may laugh when I tell you that prayer is a powerful means to building the will. You might even think that it is old-fashioned. Well, here's the reality: the warrior has practiced various forms of spiritual development over time. I do not meditate. That is just not how I am wired. I pray. But meditation, prayer, and contemplation are essential ways to improve the spiritual aspect of yourself. Physical exercise builds the spirit and reading spiritual things builds the will. My weapons of choice will always be the Bible, prayer, and physical exercise such as running or weights. This just works for me. When you strengthen the will, you are building your will-house. What a warrior understands is that belief in a higher purpose or a higher power is part of the process of the warrior's journey. Cyrus the Great, at one time the ruler of the world, acknowledged the importance of paying reverence to the Almighty God. However, if reverence is not the reason for prayer, pray because it is beneficial to your health. In fact, prayer is merely a form of meditation, but it is to be done without ceasing. Most importantly, you must train your whole person with the sole purpose of building your will to be indomitable.

WHAT IS AN IMMOVABLE MIND?

Though I am not a Zen Buddhist and adhere to a Judeo-Christian worldview, the term immovable mind comes from the word 'Fudoshin', a Buddhist term identified as:

> "The mind that remains unruffled and calm; the same imperturbable, unattached, and unfettered mind. It is the ultimate mind of mastery, achievable only through rigorous training, and equally rigorous soul-searching and spirit-forging (seishin tanren, in Japanese) through the confrontation and overcoming of our own fears and weaknesses" Stephan M. Fabian, Ph.D.).

To become indomitable, one must become immoveable. They must develop a mind that is ever moving forward toward the purpose and meaning of their life, no stopping, no hesitation. My goal for you is to become an immovable mind that stays on target. The samurai focused on developing this mind. When a swordsman developed this level of skill with the sword it is described as a mind that is fluid, it does not hesitate, it does not fixate on one thing. Rather it is focused, contained, and flows.

An immovable mind cannot be shaken, an immovable mind cannot be denied, an immoveable mind allows one to master impulse, improve mental toughness, and experience higher levels of meaning and purpose in work and life. Similarly, the Bible identifies the concept of being immovable and unshakable as essential to living a life of faithfulness and staying on the narrow road. Even in the field of sports, athletes must possess an unconquerable spirit and condition themselves to stay focused under pressure. To become immovable, you must develop the power of focus. When you improve focus, you will never be powerless to your experiences. You will learn to see experiences for what they are: just experiences. What you become is powerful.

Why I say this is because every experience can be used to increase the fire within you and everything you have gone through is meant to build that inner beast inside of you. The problem is you have to reflect on the lessons learned. How do you filter experiences? Is the experience good or bad? What you really need to focus on is this fact: every experience is temporary. But the triumph over adversity is what is remembered long after you are gone. You may not be able to change the altitude but you can change your attitude.

No matter the situation, the difference is how you view the experience, and how you will yourself to overcome it. We all know firsthand that emotions and experiences are not permanent and more times than not, feelings lie to us. They alter our perceptions and steal our confidence. But I am here to tell you that what you are today does not dictate tomorrow. Every setback does not mean you are a failure; it just means you might have to take a different direction. Sometimes it just means that in that moment or at that time of your life, you lack the required experience to arrive at your desired state. You may not have been ready for the opportunity when it came. It may not have been your time. Right now does not mean never; it simply means not right now but soon. So you can't base life on what you feel. Feelings become obstacles to your performance. Combat negative feelings with positive optimism.

HOW TO DEVELOP LEARNED OPTIMISM

"The ABCDE's of Staying Optimistic"

Martin E.P. Seligman, Ph.D., Learned Optimism: How to Change Your Mind and Your Life

Adversity

This is the problem part - write about the part of the situation that went wrong.

Beliefs

These are your beliefs about the situation. Write down how you feel about it (e.g. 'I looked stupid', or 'my wife thinks I am a failure').

Consequences

Write down what you're likely to do because of what happened. For example, you might avoid similar situations, the people who were there, or be very worried if you have to try the same thing again.

Disputation

Argue with yourself about your beliefs - most negative beliefs are overreactions. Look for other reasons why things turned out as they did.

Energy!

Notice the change in your thoughts and feelings when you successfully challenge your negative beliefs.

CHAPTER 12

LIFE IS A MARATHON

"A warrior cannot lower his head – otherwise he loses sight of the horizon of his dreams."
—PAULO COELHO

Now understand that you will experience obstacles and roadblocks on the road to renovatio. But what is important is that you recognize these are the will-building experiences that keep you moving forward even when things get hard. I remember my very first marathon. At the time my mind and my will were not as strong as today. I decided to undertake the Chicago Marathon to prove to myself that I could overcome something that seemed impossible to endure. I was not trying to break a world record, but I was trying to improve my will. This marathon was one of the most powerful experiences in my life.

I had gotten into the race as a way to begin the process of renewal, or renovatio. I spent hours training for this race. I was physically ready to run but I hadn't really prepared my mind or spirit for the grueling nature of the race. I had done the physical preparation but I had not run the race in my mind and truly committed to the journey. I felt really good on race day. Everything was going well until I hit Mile 20. At Mile 20 my knee began hurting and my mind began telling me I didn't have what it took to complete the race. I began utilizing positive self-talk to encourage myself. I told myself, "If you quit now, you will quit at everything in your life." However, I couldn't master my mind and I stopped and bent over, angry with myself. I began praying for some kind of miracle to give me the strength to continue.

My prayer was answered. As I stood leaning over, I looked up, and in the distance I could see a guy about my age; he was running toward me. His movement was slow, deliberate, and determined. He moved steadily and with purpose. But what was truly powerful about this man was that he was running with an obvious handicap. As he passed me on the street, our eyes locked and I could see that he was running with a prosthetic limb. Now, I do not know his name or what he was running for, but he moved me within my spirit and caused me to reflect on myself, my life, and who I was in that moment. My problem was that I exhibited a momentary mental handicap. When I lost faith in myself, I began to inhibit my ability to perform because I was concentrating on the pain, and not the journey. I started listening to the voice in my head that told me to stop. But the reality was that I possessed more than enough willpower to keep going. My body was not the problem. It was the mental block that I placed before me. I did not embrace the pain. I did not embrace the discomfort, and as a result I began to give in to doubt.

YOU MUST TELL YOUR BODY AND MIND THAT YOU ARE THE MASTER

When you give into the pain of an experience, allow a past failure to determine your direction, or allow your emotions to dictate the outcome of a goal, it becomes the master over you instead of you becoming the master over it. You have given your personal power away and allowed something or someone to control your destiny. You must choose who is the master and who is in servitude. We are never beaten by another; we are beaten by ourselves when we relinquish our personal power. A major reason I am in awe of the story of Esther Ann Kim is that she was a life-athlete, a warrior. She is viewed as a hero because she committed to her path and refused to deviate from it. She prepared herself to be immovable even in the face of trial. She did not let her environment dictate her destiny. She conditioned her body physically, she conditioned her mind mentally, and she developed her spirit to endure her greatest adversary. What always stands between us and our goal is ourselves. So, what do you need to tell yourself in order to overcome yourself? What do you need to tell yourself to bring you back in balance? You must be mindful and contemplate this.

USE POSITIVE SELF-TALK

Positive Self-Talk is a mental technique that builds confidence and allows you to coach your own performance. This is a method that directly impacts your mindset. You program your mind with your words. According to the author of the book, Words Can Change Your Brain, Dr. Andrew Newberg, you can transform reality with the power of your words and alter negative beliefs by what you say.

"By changing the way you use language, you change your consciousness and that in turn influences every thought, feeling, and behavior in your life."

What affirmations can you say to yourself repeatedly that will keep you motivated? What will allow you to keep going even when you want to quit? So, what can you tell yourself to keep going when the going gets tough and change seems difficult?

Here is what I tell myself:

"I am on fire"

"I am unstoppable"

"I've got this"

"I am the greatest"

"I will win"

PART 4

HARMONY – FINDING WHOLE PERSON MASTERY

CHAPTER 13

LEARNING TO BE STILL

"Be still and know that I am God."
—BIBLE

Balance or harmony is essential to optimizing human potential and realizing breakthrough performance. A key to developing mastery over yourself and improving your skill mastery is to learn to be quiet. You cannot learn to correct yourself if you are always talking. Being quiet teaches you to listen to your spirit. It teaches you to listen to the small quiet voice inside of you. You must learn to be still. Prayerful contemplation and mindfulness are techniques that are great practices to assist you in the process of improving self-awareness and they will help you move forward with the process of change. Change is realized through the process of listening to inner truth that comes from the inner voice. Contemplation is essential to improving the process of learning because it engages the metacognitive function of your brain.

Metacognition is the process of thinking about your thinking. The process of thinking about your thinking process allows you to develop self-awareness and/or increase self-awareness. What I have come to understand is that metacognition is essential to changing a behavior. To engage in the process of change requires us to assess ourselves. When we approach our day to day interactions focused on learning we are able to shift our focus and make changes to our thinking and our behaviors. It is a lot easier to change a belief by becoming aware of your thoughts than to try and change your values. Remember, when you begin to assess your thoughts, you are able to assess your beliefs and make changes in your behaviors. Here is a great model called the transtheoretical model of change that identifies the process of behavior change:

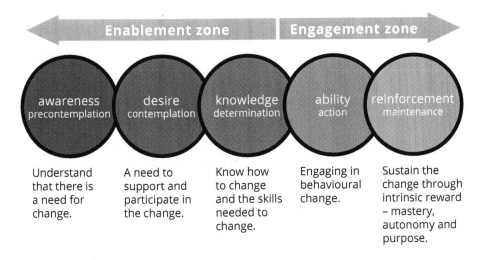

Enablement zone			Engagement zone	
awareness precontemplation	desire contemplation	knowledge determination	ability action	reinforcement maintenance
Understand that there is a need for change.	A need to support and participate in the change.	Know how to change and the skills needed to change.	Engaging in behavioural change.	Sustain the change through intrinsic reward – mastery, autonomy and purpose.

Awareness is a process of recognizing that a change is needed. This is described by Adam Smith as the ability for us to be onlookers of our own behaviors. The power of learning to be still is that it informs you about what is going on inside of you. This is linked to developing the ability to self-regulate, which is vital to developing well-being. A basic problem with many of us is that we do not know how to listen to ourselves and it inhibits our ability to change the course of our lives to work in balance or harmony with our authentic selves and not against ourselves. How many times have you set goals that you were unable to achieve because your habits were in opposition to your goals? How many times have you been unaware of a limiting belief that stopped you from achieving higher performance?

When you become mindful of your day-to-day interactions, you are able to analyze and assess yourself. I recall having a coaching session with a client who found that he would get angry and upset while in traffic. In fact, he would experience road rage every time he drove. What is interesting about him is that he did not know how to control his feelings or his irrational thinking. See, he would let his emotions rule him, and as a result he continued to repeat the same underperforming behaviors. Every day he would drive to work in a state of anger and every day he would come home angry. Of course, he blamed traffic, but the reality was he lacked self-control. His lack of self-control meant he was giving his energy away. He was giving away his personal power to external forces that he could not control because he lacked the awareness of himself, which is required to regain self-control. See, a sure sign that you are not in control of yourself is identifiable by how you react to the external environment around you. You are either controlled by it or you are in control of your person. So, let me ask you a few questions:

Are you angry when driving? Do you find yourself unable to control your tongue? Do you find yourself unable to express what you feel? Much of this has to do with you not developing the self-awareness needed to even begin the process of changing yourself. When you lack self-awareness, you give away yourself, i.e. your personal energy, and slowly you become a slave to your emotions. A warrior is not a warrior when s/he is unable to control oneself. When you lack personal mastery, it is difficult to achieve skill-mastery and his productivity as a salesman was horrible. He would come home angry every day.

In one of our sessions, I asked him why he would get so upset. His answer was that he did not know why. As our sessions progressed, we began to focus on increasing his awareness of what he was feeling, and as he began to understand the importance of developing self-awareness, he slowly began to take back his life.

You are not excused for your destructive behaviors just because you do not know why. You better find out why, because until you can understand why you do what you do, you will stay stuck in the same routine forever. So, while slavery may be a thing of the past, for some of us mental and emotional slavery is the bond we will never break until we ask ourselves why we do what we do. You can be whatever you want to be, but you can't become it until you know why you do what you do. You must learn to be conscious and stop living unconsciously. You must wake up to who you are and address the things that are a part of you but really aren't aligned with the better version of you. So, how do you develop awareness?

- Ask yourself "Why am I doing this?"
- Ask yourself "Why am I feeling like this?"
- Ask yourself "Why am I acting this way?"

The more my coachee utilized this process of questioning, it encouraged him to focus on developing conscious awareness, and slowly he began to uncover the nature of his issue. See, what you may not realize is that learning to be quiet is integral to improving performance and addressing bad behaviors. I find that many of the issues at the heart of improving performance have to do with loving ourselves enough to change the things we don't like about ourselves.

You really must learn to love yourself before you can influence others to love and accept love from others.

What is interesting about the warrior is the warrior is constantly focused on staying in touch with him or herself. The warrior takes time to be still in order to know and understand the internal dialogue that occurs in his or her mind. For my coachee, we identified that his anger was a result of being unhappy with his work. He did not love himself enough at the time to want to change himself, thereby allowing him to change his direction. What is important to understand is that love is essential to change. Do you love yourself enough to change yourself? Do you understand the power of the spirit? I attribute my renewal to my faith and the intentional development on my spirit.

Over the years I have learned to be still, I have learned to be content, and I have become aware of when I am being gripped by the spirit of anger, and I am able to check myself. This is a way of showing myself that I love myself enough to question my behaviors and work to change them. An optimal life athlete must tweak themselves if they want to live life performing at an optimal level. Do you love yourself enough to correct behaviors that stand in your way of greatness? To change your behavior requires becoming more mindful. Mindfulness is the single most powerful way to create present moment awareness. Practicing mindfulness leads to improving focus, helps to overcome addictive behaviors, it reduces stress, can help you achieve the optimal state of flow, and tap into your spirit.

Develop Mindful Awareness

Mindfulness is the act of being intensely aware of what you're sensing and feeling at every moment without interpretation or judgment.

Mental Focus Exercise

Stare at any object and try to remain focused on just that object for as long as possible. Keep a mental watch on when your mind starts to wander, then just bring it back to the object. The longer you can remain focused, the more your mindfulness will increase.

Mindful Showering

Pick an activity that constitutes part of your daily morning routine, such as brushing your teeth, shaving, making the bed, or taking a shower. When you do it, totally focus attention on what you're doing: the body movements, the taste, the touch, the smell, the sight, the sound, and so on. Notice what's happening with an attitude of openness and curiosity. For example, when you're in the shower, notice the sounds of the water as it sprays out of the nozzle, as it hits your body, and as it gurgles down the drain. Notice the temperature of the water, and the feel of it in your hair, and on your shoulders, and running down your legs. Notice the smell of the soap and shampoo, and the feel of them against your skin. Notice the sight of the water droplets on the walls or shower curtain, the water dripping down your body and the steam rising upward. Notice the movements of your arms as you wash or scrub or shampoo. When thoughts arise, acknowledge them, and let them come and go like passing cars. Again and again, you'll get caught up in your thoughts. As soon as you realize this has happened, gently acknowledge it, note what the thought was that distracted you, and immediately bring your attention back to the shower.

TAPPING INTO YOUR SPIRIT TO SEE YOUR POTENTIAL

While some may disagree, the spiritual aspect of you is critically important to your arriving at a place of harmony in your life. In his book Sharpening the Warrior's Edge, Bruce K. Siddle expresses the importance of faith and belief when he talks about soldiers in combat needing to have something to believe in in the face of war. In his view, a strong faith or belief in a higher power creates a peace of mind and minimizes the worry and anxiety common to the soldier.

Now, maybe you and I diverge on the importance of spirituality, but I bet you will agree just as I do that there is no power greater than love. Love, like no other action, can transform us. See, I have learned that abiding in faith, love, and service to others is important to transforming oneself and making a difference in the world. However, when you really think about transformation and change, they are typically inspired by an act of love for humanity or another human being; this is what heroism is.

Love, I believe, is intrinsic and it is a passion so deep that it will cause a father to run in front of a bullet to protect a child. Frankl suggests that this is a means to find meaning and I would have to agree with him. Mandela touched my heart like Frankl did some eleven years ago, and his words that I read in his autobiography stayed with me. What he stated was this:

"I always knew that deep down in every heart, there is mercy and generosity. No one is born hating. People must learn to hate, and if they can learn to hate, they can be taught to love, for love comes more naturally to the human heart than hate". See, the power of love is that it always sees the potential for greatness because perfect love drives out fear.

If it were not for love, would I be here today? Probably not. If it were not for a woman who saw something in me, I would not be here today. If it were not for the gift of love, would any of us be here today? Dr. Dennis Kimbro expressed to me that life is conceived in an act of love. Thus the greatest gift that you and I have within is our ability to abide in love. It means that when we act in a spirit of love and abide in love, we give life; but when we act in hate, we slowly take. I believe Martin Luther King, Jr. understood it, Mother Teresa understood it. When your life is fueled by the spirit of love for yourself and love for others, the greatest transformation can take place.

In my most recent conversation with Dr. Dennis Kimbro, a world-renowned speaker and author of various books on human potential, he told me how he believed the greatest social movements of our time were driven by one defining characteristic: they emphasized the spiritual power of love. So maybe it is a cliché, but it's one we so dearly need to exercise, and that is that the greatest strength of the warrior is his or her ability to love. Because when the warrior has love, he is able to conquer hate; and if the warrior is able to transform himself, then it is through the act of love that he is able to transform those around him or her. In fact, when love is exhibited by a boss to his workers, it is shown to improve their productivity. Love is a form of passion and it is a requirement that improves performance. Love is also "agape," and that is a spiritual form of love; it is the highest form of love and this type of love is transforming. So yes, I do believe that love conquers all and it is a requirement for one to show a measure of self-compassion for oneself.

In fact, self-compassion is a requirement for improving the potential for achievement. How else could Martin have accepted death for the betterment of humanity? A warrior possesses self-compassion and spiritual compassion for the world in which he operates. He recognized that some things are bigger than his life and that bigger thing is a life driven with a higher purpose. What I have learned from the greats is this: when we are engulfed in self-hate and when we experience self-denial, we cannot grow into ourselves; but when we learn to love ourselves, we are able to love others. I consider self-hate to be when we are too afraid to love ourselves enough to change our situations or circumstances, and more specifically our minds. When we do not truly love ourselves, it is difficult for our old selves to die.

One thing I know about transformation is that love is so powerful that it can alter our mental states. Here is another truth: when I started my road to renovatio, my hero's journey, it was because I was heartbroken and disillusioned about life and the state of the world I lived in. I did not understand that I could be the change the world needed, but only if I learned to love myself enough to find the warrior within me.

Before being renewed, I felt I had lost more than I thought I could bear, I had failed more times than I could count, and I regretted the past and did not believe that things would get better. But when I look back now, what I have gained is far more precious than my losses. See, my road has taken me from a place of obscurity to a place of ultimate mastery development (true mastery of anything is an illusion). What I have really lost I never wanted anyway, because a fixed mindset did not and does not agree with who I am working to become.

I lost selfishness, I lost hopelessness, and I lost the desire to seek validation from others because those are not fruits of love; they are outcomes of despair, being basic, and they are driven by fear. I have learned that perfect love drives out fear.

Love can be only the explanation for selfless acts or acts of heroism. I can only assume that it was love that allowed me to be taken in at a young age and raised by a woman who never gave birth to me. I can only attribute my story to a higher power; call it what you want, but I call Him God. I can only attribute love to being the answer. See, I hope that when I go, I will be remembered for bringing the best out of everyone with whom I came into contact. In fact, I want my funeral to be a party.

Now it sounds morbid, but I told you that the warrior must accept death so that he can savor the beauty of life. Just think about it. How much more differently would you live if you knew that tomorrow was your last day? How would you spend those moments? Would you spend them hating or loving yourself? I believe most of us would spend them loving both ourselves and others. One powerful way to cultivate the restoring power of compassion is to commit to the practice of prayer. Prayer actually releases a neurotransmitter called oxytocin in the brain. This neurotransmitter is labeled as the "love" neurotransmitter. Also, when you engage in prayer it has been shown to quiet fear, reduce anxiety, and create a state of calm. More importantly, prayer and meditation change your brains neuropathways. Why not pray? It can't hurt but it can help.

Pray For The Change You Want

Prayer can be done at any time and for anyone. Simply, close your eyes and engage your mind and heart in the act of praying. You don't have to have a special place to do it or a specific way to place your hands. You can simply pray the serenity prayer. Everyone knows this one.

"God grant us the serenity to accept the things we cannot change, the courage to change the things we can, and the wisdom to know the difference."

Here is my personal hero's prayer:

Lord give me the strength of Samson to keep my body strong, give me the wisdom of Solomon so that I may make wise decisions, give me the faith to move mountains, and the heart of a lion like David to overcome my fear today. I pray this prayer through your son Jesus Christ. Amen.

CHAPTER 14

CHOOSE TO BE HEROIC

"A hero is an ordinary individual who finds
the strength to persevere and endure in
spite of overwhelming obstacles."
—CHRISTOPHER REEVE

Now, at the beginning of this story, I discussed how as a boy I would imagine myself living heroically. Well, a hero is a warrior and heroes do heroic things, and you and I have the capacity to be heroic. Here is how. Heroism has everything to do with being selfless and courageous. A hero does something with no apparent award or reward attached to it. By the way, a hero is not born; s/he is made. More importantly, heroes focus on legacy-building activities. Heroic individuals do not live to earn a medal, but they most certainly live to make the world a better place.

As I told you in the beginning, it was always my dream to be a hero. Being heroic has everything to do with living on a higher moral plane. You could describe Martin Luther King, Jr. as heroic because he appealed to a spiritual law and his moral compass was directed toward acting justly, even when it was not popular. Heroism goes against convention, greatness goes against convention; it is countercultural. But the point is that an authentically lived life is one that is lived heroically, and to live a heroic life represents living life on the premise of serving others. But heroism is not just about service to others; it is more than being altruistic. Here is the reality: to be heroic is about being authentic and acting for the love of others, even if it costs our own lives. It is acting with morality even when everyone around us lives contrary to truth. It is living with higher virtues; a warrior is identified as a hero because s/he lives for more than oneself. This is the ideal that has always stuck with me about greatness: it is a lifelong commitment to better yourself and bettering humanity.

What does being heroic entail? According to Philip Zimbardo, the world-renowned psychologist:

1. First, heroism involves some type of quest.
2. Second, heroism must have some form of actual or anticipated sacrifice or risk.
3. Third, the heroic act can either be passive or active.
4. Finally, heroism can be a sudden, one-time act, or something that persists over a longer period of time.

So, are you heroic? Well, you just might be. But that is for you to find out.

Mihaly Csikszentmihalyi suggests that the greatest value is created in the moments when we are able to control our innermost knowledge or our inner person. When we have control of what's inside of us, we can address the obstacles outside of us. The true goal of the warrior is to live in harmony or balance with himself. Mihaly believes that in order to experience joy, an optimal state of inner control over the mind is essential to experiencing happiness in life. Because joy is found when we learn to control this inner life, a focus on mastering the mind, the body, and the emotions is essential to living a more engaged, meaningful, and fearless way of life. You may know the term as "no pain, no gain."

You may be shocked to know that Muhammed Ali actually hated training, but he did it to be the greatest of all-time. In fact, he stated, "I hated every minute of training, but I said, 'Don't quit. Suffer now and live the rest of your life as a champion.'"

See, I think happiness is not a result of taking the easy road. Rather it is the result of living a life aligned with your values and being authentic in expressing your emotions, in an attempt to overcome yourself and achieve personal growth. I think Viktor Frankl is right when he suggests that only when the emotions work in terms of values can the individual feel pure joy. Stop looking for happiness, it is a byproduct of living a life of meaning.

Meaning is what drives you toward your purpose, and when you are living from a place of purpose, you will be right-aligned to be more, do more, and achieve more. The warrior develops mastery over the inner life to exert power over the mundane and ordinary world outside. Because life is about optimizing experiences, finding the hidden gem in the experiences is how you optimize life and perform at an elite level. Similarly, when you take the time to develop your inner warrior by seeking to understand the significance of the moments in your life, you are acquiring the weapons needed for the warrior to just get on with the hero's journey -- the road to renovatio. Don't stop at being a great performer in work and life; begin to turn your attention toward being a great and loving human being. This is the ultimate mastery and it is something beautiful.

St. Augustine stated this about people:

> *"Men go abroad to wonder at the heights of mountains, and the huge long courses of the rivers, at the vast compass of the ocean, at the circular motions of the stars, and they pass by themselves without wondering."*

Do you realize the most beautiful creation, the greatest work of art, was when the Creator created you? So, why are you passing by yourself either never wondering, or wondering with no true motivation to understand who you really are, what you are really capable of, and how you can make a lasting impact on the world around you? You must be in balance, you must live with a purpose, because you were not born by accident but for divine purpose. See, as you learn to exercise authority over yourself, you will have the capability to lead others and leave a legacy behind that will be remembered long after you are gone, and that is heroic. It is time for you to leave your legacy.

One last truth I want to share with you: I promised myself the day my father died that I would work to become a beautiful man. I am not perfect; like you, I have a long way to go. But I made my choice to take the road to renovatio.

CONCLUSION

TAKE THE PATH

"The path of the Warrior is lifelong, and mastery is often simply staying on the path."

—RICHARD STROZZI HECKLER

May you walk your road to the finish, may you run with careless abandon, and live well, my dear warrior. Run your race as if for a purpose. Commit to being the best version of yourself each day. Abide in love and let the little ember of fire slowly flicker; may it become a flame because eventually it too will fade, and like every star that dies become a supernova. So, burn hot and shine for all the world to see. Now it is your turn to write your story, your magnus opus, your greatest work. PUSH on to the upward call. Your mountain is waiting. Now, which road will you choose? I chose to take the road to renovatio.

Just know this, every average man makes a choice to become a warrior; every warrior can't be the hero, and not everyone has the courage to take the path with heart. Which road will you choose? Like Robert Frost, I have chosen to take the road less traveled and I am all the better for it. Be courageous and do not fear for God is with you.

So, I leave you with these final words:

Dear warrior,

After reading this book, you've grown stronger than you could've imagined. The only way to know how strong you are is for you to keep testing your limits. You will give people an ideal to strive towards. They will race behind you; you will stumble and they will stumble; you will fall and at times they will fall. But in time, they will join you in the sun, dear warrior. In time, you will help them accomplish wonders and you will accomplish wonders.

You have everything inside of you to become an optimal life athlete. So, live each day as if it is your last. For a warrior does not fear living, he fears not reaching his ultimate potential. And that is ultimate mastery.

NOTES

Introduction: My Road To Renovatio

1. Merriam-webster Dictionary. Springfield, MA: Merriam-Webster, 2000. Internet resource. Used to define the word rebirth and renewal.
2. Frankl, Viktor E., and Ilse Lasch. Man's Search for Meaning An Introd. to Logotherapy. Boston: Beacon, 1963. Print. Frankl identifies man must take responsibility for his life.
3. Kübler-Ross, Elisabeth. On Death and Dying. , 1969. Print. Dr. Ross identifies the stages of grief.
4. Divine, Mark. The Way of the Seal: Think Like an Elite Warrior to Lead and Succeed. , 2013. Print. Talks about the importance of developing self-mastery.

Chapter 1: Becoming A Hero

5. Lee, Bruce, and John R. Little. Striking Thoughts: Bruce Lee's Wisdom for Daily Living. Boston: Tuttle Pub., 2000. Print.
6. Jung, Carl "Psychology and Religion" (1938). In CW 11: Psychology and Religion: West and East. p.131.

7. Lee, Bruce, and John R. Little. Striking Thoughts: Bruce Lee's Wisdom for Daily Living. Boston: Tuttle Pub., 2000. Print "Successful man develops laser focus.

8. Myss, Caroline M. Archetypes: Who Are You? Carlsbad, CA: Hay House, 2013. Print. Identifies what archetypes are.

9. Spencer, Robert L. The Craft of the Warrior. Berkeley, CA: Frog, 1993. Print.

10. Snyder, Zack, Charles Roven, Christopher Nolan, Emma Thomas, Deborah Snyder, David S. Goyer, Henry Cavill, Amy Adams, Michael Shannon, Kevin Costner, Diane Lane, Laurence Fishburne, Russell Crowe, and Hans Zimmer. Man of Steel. Burbank, CA: Warner Home Video, 2013. Dialogue with superman and his father.

11. Campbell, Joseph. The Hero with a Thousand Faces. Princeton, NJ: Princeton UP, 1972. Print.

12. Spencer, Robert L. The Craft of the Warrior. Berkeley, CA: Frog, 1993. Print. "The core of the modern warrior myth" p.25

13. Myss, Caroline M. Archetypes: Who Are You? Carlsbad, CA: Hay House, 2013. Print. Warrior is representative of physical and emotional strength.

14. Castaneda, Carlos. The Teachings of Don Juan: A Yaqui Way of Knowledge. Berkeley: University of California Press, 1968. Print

15. Klemmer, Brian. The Compassionate Samurai: Being Extraordinary in an Ordinary World. Carlsbad, CA: Hay House, Inc, 2008. Print. Man is a three part snowman spirit, body, and soul.

16. Lee, Bruce, and John R. Little. Striking Thoughts: Bruce Lee's Wisdom for Daily Living. Boston: Tuttle Pub., 2000. Print. Talks about the force of the spirit.

17. Bolelli, Daniele. On the Warrior's Path: Fighting, Philosophy, and Martial Arts Mythology. Berkeley, Calif: Frog, Ltd, 2003. Print. Bolelli identifies who Musashi was.

18. Moon, Young K, Eun J. Kim, and Yeong-Mahn You. "Study on Expertise Development Process Based on Arête." International Journal of Information and Education Technology. (2013): 226-230. Print. Discussed the meta model of expertise.

Chapter 2: A Mentored Mind

19. Ericsson, K A. Peak: Secrets from the New Science of Expertise. , 2016. Print.

20. Xenophon, and Larry Hedrick. Xenophon's Cyrus the Great: The Arts of Leadership and War. New York: Truman Talley /Saint Martin's, 2006. Print. p.3.

21. Marcus, Aurelius, George Long, and Aurelius Marcus. The Meditations. Mineola, N.Y: Dover Publications, 1997. Internet resource.

22. Bandura, Albert. Social Learning Theory. Englewood Cliffs, N.J: Prentice Hall, 1977. Print. Identifies the social learning theory.

23. Lee, Bruce, and John R. Little. Striking Thoughts: Bruce Lee's Wisdom for Daily Living. Boston: Tuttle Pub., 2000. Print. Bruce identifies what truth is on page 203.

24. Kaufman, Steve, and Musashi Miyamoto. Musashi's Book of Five Rings: The Definitive Interpretation of Miyamoto Musashi's Classic Book of Strategy. Boston: Tuttle Pub., 2004. Print. One must understand the inner and outer.

25. Peabody, Josephine P. Old Greek Folk Stories Told Anew. Boston: Houghton, Mifflin, 1897. Print. Story of Icarus.

26. Greene, Robert. Mastery. New York: Viking, 2012. Print. Identifies how to attain mastery.

27. Kaufman, Steve, and Musashi Miyamoto. Musashi's Book of Five Rings: The Definitive Interpretation of Miyamoto Musashi's Classic Book of Strategy. Boston: Tuttle Pub., 2004. Print. Cautions against taking the journey of mastery alone.

28. Lee, Bruce, and John R. Little. Striking Thoughts: Bruce Lee's Wisdom for Daily Living. Boston: Tuttle Pub., 2000. Print. Bruce on self-knowledge see p.181.

Chapter 3: A Lesson On Stars

29. Frankl, Viktor E., and Ilse Lasch. Man's Search for Meaning An Introd. to Logotherapy. Boston: Beacon, 1963. Print.

30. Canda, Edward R. Spiritual Diversity and Social Work: A Comprehensive Bibliography with Annotations. Alexandria: Council on Social Work Education, 2003. Print.

31. Maslow, Abraham H. The Farthest Reaches of Human Nature. Penguin, 1976. Print.

32. Nee, Watchman. 1968. The spiritual man. New York: Christian Fellowship Publishers Inc. Nee identifies the inward man and outward man.

33. Loehr, James E, and Tony Schwartz. The Power of Full Engagement: Managing Energy, Not Time, Is the Key to High Performance and Personal Renewal. New York: Free Press, 2003. Print.

34. Csikszentmihalyi, Mihaly. Flow: The Psychology of Optimal Experience. New York: Harper & Row, 1990. Print.

35. Engstrom, Ted W. The Pursuit of Excellence. Grand Rapids, Mich: Zondervan Pub. House, 1982. Print

36. MacLean, Paul D. The Triune Brain in Evolution: Role in Paleocerebral Functions. New York: Plenum Press, 1990. Print.

37. Schwartz, Jeffrey, and Rebecca Gladding. You Are Not Your Brain: The 4-Step Solution for Changing Bad Habits, Ending Unhealthy Thinking, and Taking Control of Your Life. New York: Avery, 2012. Print.

38. Mandela, Nelson. Long Walk to Freedom: The Autobiography of Nelson Mandela. Boston: Little, Brown, 1994. Print. Nelson and his daily exercise see page 322.

Chapter 4: Back To A Lesson On Stars

39. Sterner, Thomas M. The Practicing Mind: Developing Focus and Discipline in Your Life : Master Any Skill or Challenge by Learning to Love the Process. Novato, Calif: New World Library, 2012. Print.

40. Pearson, Karl. The Life, Letters, and Labours of Francis Galton. Cambridge: University Press, 1914. Print.

41. Ericsson, K A. Peak: Secrets from the New Science of Expertise. , 2016. Print.

42. Miller, Patricia, and Gretchen Kerr. "Conceptualizing Excellence: Past, Present, and Future." Journal of Applied Sport Psychology. 14.3 (2002): 140-153. Print.

43. Frankl, Viktor E. The Will to Meaning: Foundations and Applications of Logotherapy. New York: World Pub. Co, 1969. Print.

44. Frankl, Victor (1988). The Will to Meaning: Foundations and Applications of Logotherapy. New York, NY: Penguin Books.

45. Csikszentmihalyi, Mihaly. Flow: The Psychology of Optimal Experience. New York: Harper & Row, 1990. Print.

46. Marden, Orison S. An Iron Will. Waiheke Island: Floating Press, 2008. Internet resource.

47. Moneta, Giovanni B. Positive Psychology: A Critical Introduction. , 2014. Print. Ryff scale of psychological wellbeing chart.

48. Johnson, Monte Ransome. Aristotle on Teleology. : Oxford University Press, 2005-11-03. Oxford Scholarship Online. 2006-02-01. Date Accessed 20 Jan. 2017 <http://www.oxfordscholarship.com/view/10.1093/0199285306.001.0001/acprof-9780199285303>.

Chapter 5: Why Meaning is Important To You

49. Engstrom, Ted W. The Pursuit of Excellence. Grand Rapids, Mich: Zondervan Pub. House, 1982. Print

50. Csikszentmihalyi, Mihaly. Flow: The Psychology of Optimal Experience. New York: Harper & Row, 1990. Print.

51. Maslow, Abraham H. Religions, Values, and Peak-Experiences. New York: Penguin Arkana, 1994. Print. Peak experiences research.

52. Torrance, Robert M. The Spiritual Quest: Transcendence in Myth, Religion, and Science. Berkeley: University of California Press, 1994. Internet resource. Vision Quest (p.264) Journal. 33.4 (1990): 692-724. Print.) Spiritual vision of young Indians.

53. "Gallup (2013). State of the Global Workplace: Employee Engagement Insights for Business Leaders Worldwide. Retrieved from www.gallup.com, www.healthways.com

54. Kahn, W A. "Psychological Conditions of Personal Engagement and Disengagement at Work." Academy of Management.

55. The Holy Bible: New American Standard Bible. New York: American Bible Society, 1991. Print. See proverbs 18:16.

56. Kaufman, Steve, and Musashi Miyamoto. Musashi's Book of Five Rings: The Definitive Interpretation of Miyamoto Musashi's Classic Book of Strategy. Boston: Tuttle Pub., 2004. Print. Musashi quote on "nothing exists outside of you.

57. Wimbush, Vincent L, and Richard Valantasis. Asceticism. New York: Oxford University Press, 2002. Internet resource. Asceticism. Research on the ascetic.

58. Baumeister, Roy F, and John Tierney. Willpower: Rediscovering the Greatest Human Strength. New York: Penguin Press, 2011. Print.

59. Frankl, Viktor E. The Will to Meaning: Foundations and Applications of Logotherapy. New York: World Pub. Co, 1969. Print. Frankl identifies the various types of will humans have.

60. Csikszentmihalyi, Mihaly. Flow: The Psychology of Optimal Experience. New York: Harper & Row, 1990. Print. Discusses a unified "flow" experience on page 217.

61. Frankl, Viktor E., and Ilse Lasch. Man's Search for Meaning An Introd. to Logotherapy. Boston: Beacon, 1963. Print.

62. Marx, Karl, Max Eastman, Julian Borchardt, Vladimir I. Lenin, Karl Marx, and Karl Marx. Capital, the Communist Manifesto, and Other Writings. New York: Modern Library, 1932. Print.

Chapter 6: Do You Know Your Potential?

63. Drucker, Peter F, and Deaver Brown. Managing Oneself. , 2014. Internet resource.

64. Gardner, S. (n.d.). Study Focuses on Strategies for Achieving Goals, Resolutions. Retrieved January 01, 2018, from

www.dominican.edu/dominicannews/study-highlights-strategies-for-achieving-goals. Dominican University of California, Dr. Gail Matthews Goals Research.

65. Kent, Richard. "Learning from Athletes' Writing: Creating Activity Journals." The English Journal, vol. 104, no. 1, 2014, pp. 68–74. JSTOR, JSTOR, www.jstor.org/stable/24484354. Details how Serena Williams and Michael Phelps journal to achieve optimal performance.

66. Pennebaker, James W, and John F. Evans. Expressive Writing: Words That Heal. , 2014. Print. James Pennebaker talks about the health benefits of journaling.

67. Dweck, Carol S. Mindset: The New Psychology of Success. New York: Random House, 2006. Print.

68. David, Daniel, Steven J. Lynn, and Albert Ellis. Rational and Irrational Beliefs: Research, Theory, and Clinical Practice. New York: Oxford University Press, 2010. Print.

69. Flanagan, Eileen. The Wisdom to Know the Difference: When to Make a Change-and When to Let Go. New York: Jeremy P. Tarcher/Penguin, 2009. Print.

70. Ungerleider, Steven. Mental Training for Peak Performance: Top Athletes Reveal the Mind Exercises They Use to Excel. Emmaus, Penn: Rodale, 2005. Print. Visualization techniques.

71. Ranganathan, Vinoth & Siemionow, Vlodek & Liu, Jingzhi & Sahgal, Vinod & Yue, Guang. (2004). From Mental Power to Muscle Power—Gaining Strength by Using the Mind. Neuropsychologia. 42. 944-56. 10.1016/j.neuropsychologia.2003.11.018. Study showed that the mind can be used to make muscle growth.

72. Pascual-Leone, Alvaro & Nguyet, D & Cohen, L.G. & Brasil-Neto, Joaquim & Cammarota, A & Hallett, M. (1995). Modulation of Muscle Responses Evoked by Transcranial Magnetic Stimulation

during the Acquisition of New Fine Motor Skills. Journal of neurophysiology. 74. 1037-45.10.1152/jn.1995.74.3.1037.

73. Frankl, Viktor E., and Ilse Lasch. Man's Search for Meaning An Introd. to Logotherapy. Boston: Beacon, 1963. Print.

74. Ichaso, León, John Penotti, Fisher Stevens, Tim Williams, John Leguizamo, Kathy DeMarco, Benjamin Bratt, Giancarlo Esposito, Talisa Soto, Nelson Vasquez, Michael Wright, Michael Irby, Mandy Patinkin, Robert Klein, Rita Moreno, Claudio Chea, David Tedeschi, Sharon Lomofsky, Kip Hanrahan, and Sandra Hernandez. Piñero. , 2002. Poem seeking the cause.

75. Weinzweig, Ari, Ian Nagy, and Ryan Stiner. A Lapsed Anarchist's Approach to Managing Ourselves. Ann Arbor: Zingerman's Press, 2013. Print. See page 231-232.

Chapter 7: Fear of Living

76. "Gallup (2013). State of the Global Workplace: Employee Engagement Insights for Business Leaders Worldwide. Retrieved from www.gallup.com, www.healthways.com

77. Lee, Bruce, and John R. Little. Striking Thoughts: Bruce Lee's Wisdom for Daily Living. Boston: Tuttle Pub., 2000. Print. Limiting yourself.

78. Spencer, Robert L. The Craft of the Warrior. Berkeley, CA: Frog, 1993. Print. Impeccability.

79. Bryant, Andrew, and Ana L. Kazan. Self-leadership: How to Become a More Successful, Efficient, and Effective Leader from the Inside Out. New York: McGraw-Hill, 2013. Print

Chapter 8: Death Awakens The Warrior

80. Ansbro, John J. Martin Luther King, Jr: The Making of a Mind. Maryknoll, N.Y: Orbis Books, 1982. Print

81. Greenberg, J., Pyszczynski, T., Solomon, S., Rosenblatt, A., Veeder, M., Kirkland, S., et al. (1990). Evidence for terror management, II: The effects of mortality salience on reactions to those who threaten or bolster the cultural worldview. Journal of Personality and Social Psychology, 58, 308-318.

82. Werdel, Mary B, and Robert J. Wicks. Primer on Posttraumatic Growth: An Introduction and Guide. Hoboken, N.J: John Wiley & Sons, 2012. Internet resource. Post traumatic growth.

83. On the Back of an Asian Elephant (elephas Maximus) – the Backside of the Elephant Tourism with Focus on Welfare. SLU/Dept. of Animal Environment and Health, 2014. Internet resource. Elephant crushing.

Chapter 9: The Warrior Learns To Be Courageous

84. Mandela, Nelson. Long Walk to Freedom: The Autobiography of Nelson Mandela. Boston: Little, Brown, 1994. Print. See page 622 Mandela talks about what courage is.

85. C. G. Jung, Aion in The Collected Works of C. G. Jung, ed. William McGuire et al., trans. R. F. C. Hull, Bollingen Series XX (Princeton, N.J.: Princeton University Press, 1954-79) Vol. 9/2, p. 10.

86. Chan, Francis, and Danae Yankoski. Crazy Love: Overwhelmed by a Relentless God. Colorado Springs, Colo: David C. Cook, 2008. Print.

87. Frankl, Viktor E., and Ilse Lasch. Man's Search for Meaning An Introd. to Logotherapy. Boston: Beacon, 1963. Print.

88. Wilson, William S. The Lone Samurai: The Life of Miyamoto Musashi. , 2013. Internet resource.

89. Weinzweig, Ari, Ian Nagy, and Ryan Stiner. A Lapsed Anarchist's Approach to Managing Ourselves. Ann Arbor: Zingerman's Press, 2013. Print. See page 231-232.

90. Csikszentmihalyi, Mihaly. Creativity: Flow and the Psychology of Discovery and Invention. New York: HarperCollinsPublishers, 1996. Print.

91. Kaufman, Steve, and Musashi Miyamoto. Musashi's Book of Five Rings: The Definitive Interpretation of Miyamoto Musashi's Classic Book of Strategy. Boston: Tuttle Pub., 2004. Print.

92. Fields, Rick. The Awakened Warrior: Living with Courage, Compassion & Discipline. New York: Putnam, 1994. Print. Dan Millman p.18.

93. Irving, Washington. Rip Van Winkle. Raleigh, N.C: Alex Catalogue, 1990. Internet resource.

Chapter 10: From Fear To Power

94. Kaufman, Steve, and Musashi Miyamoto. Musashi's Book of Five Rings: The Definitive Interpretation of Miyamoto Musashi's Classic Book of Strategy. Boston: Tuttle Pub., 2004. Print.

95. Lee, Bruce, and John R. Little. Striking Thoughts: Bruce Lee's Wisdom for Daily Living. Boston: Tuttle Pub., 2000. Print. Will makes a man see page 63.

96. "Armstrong, Lance, and Sally Jenkins. It's Not About the Bike: My Journey Back to Life. New York: Putnam, 2000. Print. Lance quote when I feel like quitting.

97. Afremow, James A. The Champion's Mind: How Great Athletes Think, Train, and Thrive. , 2013. Print. In champions mind he suggests focusing on what you can control.

98. Dreyfus S., Dreyfus H. (1980), A five-stage model of the mental activities involved in directed skill acquisition, California University Berkeley Operations Research Center. http://www. dtic.mil/dtic/index.html (access: Feb. 2, 2016)

99. Ido Movement for Culture. Journal of Martial Arts Anthropology, 2000. [online], Stowarzyszenie Idokan Polska. [Accessed 18 February 2018]. Retrieved from: http://www. idokan.pl/ Shu-Ha-Ri model.

100. W.C. Howell and E.A. Fleishman (eds.), Human Performance and Productivity. Vol 2: Information Processing and Decision Making. Hillsdale, NJ: Erlbaum; 1982. Conscious Competency model.

Chapter 11: Stay The Course

101. Gabriel, Richard A. Hannibal : The Military Biography Of Rome's Greatest Enemy. Washington, D.C.: Potomac Books, 2011. eBook Academic Collection (EBSCOhost). Web. 23 Jan. 2017. Hannibal

102. The Holy Bible: New American Standard Bible. New York: American Bible Society, 1991. Print. See Corinthians 2:11.

103. Takuan, Sōhō, and William S. Wilson. The Unfettered Mind: Writings of the Zen Master to the Sword Master. Tokyo: Kodansha International, 1986. Print. Understanding the immoveable mind.

104. Seligman, Martin E. P. Learned Optimism. North Sydney, N.S.W: William Heinemann Australia, 2011. Print.

Chapter 12: Life is A Marathon

105. Chan, Francis, and Danae Yankoski. Crazy Love: Overwhelmed by a Relentless God. Colorado Springs, Colo: David C. Cook, 2008. Print.

106. Newberg, Andrew B, and Mark R. Waldman. Words Can Change Your Brain: 12 Conversation Strategies to Build Trust, Resolve Conflict, and Increase Intimacy. New York: Plume, 2013. Print. See page 35.

Chapter 13: Learning To Be Still

107. Analysis of the Transtheoretical Model of Behavior Change. , 2011. Internet resource.

108. Smith, Adam, and Dugald Stewart. The Theory of Moral Sentiments, Or, an Essay Towards an Analysis of the Principles by Which Men Naturally Judge Concerning the Conduct and Character, First of Their Neighbours, and Afterwards of Themselves, to Which Is Added a Dissertation on the Origin of Languages. London: Henry G. Bohn, 2013. Internet resource.

109. Grenville-Cleave, Bridget. Positive Psychology: A Practical Guide. London: Icon Books, 2012. Internet resource. Discusses mindfulness techniques.

Chapter 14: Choose To Be The Hero

110. Siddle, Bruce K. Sharpening the Warrior's Edge. Belleville, Ill: Distributed by PPCT Research Publications, PPCT Management Systems, 1995. Print.

111. Mandela, Nelson. Long Walk to Freedom: The Autobiography of Nelson Mandela. Boston: Little, Brown, 1994. Print. See page 622 on the love.

112. Newberg, Andrew B, and Mark R. Waldman. How God Changes Your Brain: Breakthrough Findings from a Leading Neuroscientist. New York: Ballantine Books Trade Paperbacks, 2010. Print.

113. "Serenity Prayer" written by Reinhold Niebuhr (1892-1971)

114. Zimbardo,Philip. What Makes a Hero http://greatergood. berkeley.edu/article/item/what_makes_a_hero/

115. Csikszentmihalyi, Mihaly. Flow: The Psychology of Optimal Experience. New York: Harper & Row, 1990. Print.

116. Augustine, , William Watts, John Norton, John Partridge, and James Laurie. Saint Augustines Confessions. London: Printed by Iohn Norton, for Iohn Partridge, 1631. Print.

ABOUT THE AUTHOR

Dr. Michael D. Amos, PsyD, PCC., is a doctor of psychology, author, speaker, coach, and entrepreneur. He is the founder of Renovatio Leadership Institute, a training institute for the development of Optimal human performance and self-leadership development. He is high energy and inquisitive about the power of mind, body, and spirit. He studies how humans can overcome their mental barriers to succeed under extreme conditions and thrive by adopting mental toughness. He is on a mission to empower humans and organizations to achieve optimal functioning to improve the quality of work and life. Mike is also passionate about studying warrior cultures, diverse aspects of psychology, neuroscience, entrepreneurship and leadership.

Dr. Mike is married to Christina Amos and enjoys hanging out with their Chihuahua, Shorty.

If you would like to contact the author, he would love to hear from you. For more information, visit Michaeldamos.com or Renovat-io.com or send an email to: mike@renovat-io.com.

ACKNOWLEDGMENTS

There are many people to thank. First, I would like to thank God for His love and protection. He will always be my eternal father. I would like to thank Roxie Williams for literally saving my life when I was a child. I would like to thank my care givers Joyce and Ivory Williams for taking me in and instilling in me a fear of God, encouraging me to take risks, and teaching me how to channel my mind into productive pursuits.

I would like to thank my wife, Christina Amos, my sister, and brothers for their encouragement and emotional support. I would like to thank Dr. Timothy Emerick for his weekly conversations with me over the last six years, Ari Weinzweig for his mentorship on business, life, and book writing, my father-in-law, Norbert Metzler, for his spiritual counsel and fatherly example, and German Cadena for his influence in the early years of my life when I was lost. Lastly, I want to thank my warrior coachees for being my test group for my ideas and working hard every day to be more, do more, and achieve more.

May this book be a blessing to each and every one of you and a manual to guide you on your Road To Renovatio.

Sincerely,

RECOMMENDED READING

Mastery

Leonard, George. (1992). Mastery: The keys to success and long-term fulfillment. New York, etc.: Plume.

Elite Minds

Beecham, Stan. 2017. Elite Minds: how winners think differently to create a competitive edge and maximize success.

The Monk Who Sold His Ferrari

Sharma, Robin S. 2015. The Monk Who Sold His Ferrari: a spiritual fable about fulfilling your dreams and reaching your destiny.

The Power of Full Engagement

Loehr, James E. 2017. The Power of Full Engagement: managing energy, not time, is the key to high performance and personal renewal.

Grit

Duckworth, Angela L., Christopher Peterson, Michael D. Matthews, and Dennis R. Kelly. 2007. "Grit: Perseverance and passion for long-term goals".

The Mindful Athlete

Mumford, George. 2016. The Mindful Athlete: secrets to pure performance.

A Lapsed Anarchist's Approach to Managing Ourselves

Weinzweig, Ari, Ian Nagy, and Ryan Stiner. 2013. A Lapsed Anarchist's Approach to Managing Ourselves. Ann Arbor: Zingerman's Press.

Off Balance on Purpose

Thurmon, Dan. 2010. Off Balance on Purpose: embrace uncertainty and create a life you love. Austin, Texas: Greenleaf.

The Craft of the Warrior

Spencer, Robert L. The Craft of the Warrior. Berkeley, CA: Frog, 1993. Print.

Striking Thoughts

Lee, Bruce, and John R. Little. Striking Thoughts: Bruce Lee's Wisdom for Daily Living. Boston: Tuttle Pub., 2000.

The Way of the Seal

Divine, Mark. The Way of the Seal: Think Like an Elite Warrior to Lead and Succeed. , 2013. Print. Talks about the importance of developing self-mastery.